The Importance of the Protection and Integration of the Environment

Recovering the relation connection and integration between human beings and the environment for the present and future.

Fatima K. Hosein

Table of Contents

Introduction

Since the beginning of history, there has existed an important connection between the environment and human beings which has been suffering negative changes and losses in their connection, their relation, and even loss and diminution in the respect from human beings to the environment, causing unprecedented changes in the world in different ways, affecting life, progress, and possibilities of advancements.

Many changes, and transitions, through time have the environment seen in the world, even much more before human beings, and even before all the existent transformations, and exigencies of human beings, as the advancements produced by technology, industries, and business, and all the diverse aspects of life.

- ✓ What are the changes and advancements that the environment has to pay for?

It can be said at the cost of life, damaging and killing our environment, the environment of all living beings in the world, causing death and changes in all environments and living being cycles, when part of society, institutions, and international organizations try to protect the environment, of the world (our home) they have to overcome a great number of challenges due they constitute a minor part of all human beings, institutions, organizations, and businesses that are part of the world.

The lack of knowledge and/or interest in the environment is being produced as a consequence of the separation of feeling and connections that once existed between human beings and the environment, between human beings and animals it represents one of the challenges and areas of failure of that all the sectors of society, and human being need to surpass.

- ✓ How and when did that connection get lost?
- ✓ How will it be possible to recover that connection with the environment, animals, plants, and life?
- ✓ Is it too late to recover that lost connection?

No never is too late, but it will require a little effort, courage, love, and willpower from all to recover that essence, the lack of knowledge, the diminution of education in school, the loss of connection with the environment, loss of sensitivity are some of the challenges that are present in every step, in every action, and in every activity that will be taken to recover the connection with the environment, animals, and life, not forgetting the most important thing is to not give up and always continue walking on this path of love and interest for life, always remembering that environment is part of us and us are part of the environment, and this part of the journey it is accompanied with a challenge that is directed into the protection and integration with the environment, and how to recover that connection with the environment that was lost.

There is no doubt that it will encounter many challenges, questions, doubt, and even a contradiction of feelings, but all of them will have an answer, a solution, and satisfaction as it will be encountering a way to use and apply strategies, mechanisms, and even ideas that already exist, with the creation and implementation of new strategies, mechanisms, and ideas that will generate success and results capable of survive on time present and future getting involve every day more and more people, institutions, organization, business around the world.

Diverse aspects, situations, and events accompanied with questions that will increase the defiance that exists and create the opportunity to create and implement actions and strategies to change the actual situation, such as reducing the distance and limitations, implementing sanctions to those who don't comply with the obligations and responsibilities established in the national and international legislations.

Environment

Today many authors, researchers, professionals, and scientists have written and published books about environments, information, and cases that go from the most simple to the most theoretical and complex using also a language making it capable so everyone is capable of reading and managing that information, but this book is not focused on that type of information of presenting definitions, or explanations about the meaning scientific or professional/technical terms, languages or study about the environment is about to understand the importance, connection, and protection with and for the environment, and for that, the definition or explanation with which is going to be explained and referred to the environment is:

Environment = Life

The environment secrets, enigmas, beauty, and challenges that exist are the reason for studies, research, and publications in books, magazines, and papers, as also has been the inspiration for movies, showing and demonstrating the good and bad, positive and negative impact that the environment has, have and will suffer due the actions and omissions of the human being.

In actuality, it is possible to encounter numerous definitions related to the environment in dictionaries, books, papers, research, discussions, and debates all and everyone with a different perspective but sharing the same objective to understand what the environment is, why is important, and explain it to the society, in general, using technical/professional and no technical/professional language open the possibilities to reach to everyone. A few examples, of the definitions that are presented in a general and simple way and as also encountered in dictionaries such as Oxford Languages and Britannica refer to the environment as:

"…the surroundings or conditions in which
a person, animal, or plant lives or
operates…"

"…the natural world…"

"…the natural world, as a whole or in a
particular geographical area, especially as
affected by human activity…"

An important unknown aspect regarding the environment, and contrary to what many people think or believe about his meaning, environment is life, it also has feelings and gives protection to all living beings, to those that can be seen with a simple eye and to those that are so small that only can be viewed with a microscope. Researchers, authors, scientists, and professionals in the area have provided multiple and diverse definitions of environment, definitions that have kept their essence in time, which is also have been subject to adaptations or modifications so it will be capable of understanding and explaining to all what the environment, to understand the diversity and changes of the environment, with no doubt that is a complex subject, sometimes difficult, and full of challenges due that environment as living being for the professionals, experts, researchers in the area and for those who are not expert and dedicated to the study of the environment demonstrating that is not static, is always changing, transforming, but also is suffering the consequences of human being actions and omissions.

The complexity, diversity, and essence of the environment are known as the life of the world, which carries inside secrets, and mysteries that for many years researchers, and scientists, have tried to discover, and understand, but every time they feel or believe that are getting closer or near to discover their secrets they encounter something else completely different that they haven't seen, or considered before, something that grown the intrigue, doubts, and questions, as well as to increase the curiosity to discover and understand, that new discovering it doesn't stop them by contrary they feel it as a challenge where have two options, one to accept the challenge and continue studying, doing research, surpassing obstacles and the second option is to not accept the challenge and give up and consider that is not worth understanding and knowing the environment that surrounds all human beings, all life in the world.

An interesting discussion happens in all the sectors that are involved directly and not directly in the origin of the environment, a point in which it is necessary to consider the events, situations, time, actions, and omissions that have occurred even when is thought that it doesn't have relevance or relation to the environment it will be surprised how everything is related and every action or omission has a direct effect on the environment no matter where those situations, events actions or omissions occur, it will affect all environment and all living creating the necessity and obligation to all human being, business government politics international organizations, institutions, professionals, researchers, scientists not only to a specific group to reach a common or equal position regarding the environment.

The birth of sides regarding the environment has created positions where some say that sides see the environment as static, others as in constant change far from being static, or probably because of the location, particularities of the territory or locations, but the true is that even when they can share some points in accordance never will be in complete accordance in all the aspects regarding the environment.

Environment means life, it always has existed and will continue being present even after human death a belief that human beings have is that they can affect the environment and not suffer the consequences or it will not affect all life that exists in the world, the consequences and effects that will suffer all living doing not have any distinction, including the economics, political position, situations that carry to one same point which is that understanding the environment is not easy is very complex, different and ample. Since the beginning of times, scientists have conducted studies, research, investigations, and analyses, that have produced adaptations, emerging new definitions, elements, data, information, and debates in the theoretical and practical field, considering the past and emerging new information, capable of generating a new change, a new pattern has merged making necessary to make new studies, new analyses, new research, to help understand this new pattern.

Another side completely different from the scientific, and legal considerations of the environment, is there also the side of tales, legends, the stories that can and are told by the ancestors, tribes, and Indigenous around the world, which have been capable of surviving through time passing from generations to generations demonstrating until today, but there they are not only tales, legends or stories they are the connection of the environment with all living beings, how is important to live and how today human being has lost part of that connection with the environment. The only word that defines environment it covers all definitions, elements, characteristics, events, and situations that surround the environment.

- ✓ How it is possible that the environment can be related to life, and cover all the different aspects of the environment?

At this point is possible to refer to three groups, the first group says that is not possible, is not correct, or even is against all scientific research theoretical and practice knowledge and information, the second group says that is a complete lack of knowledge, and a third group react to this subject with the question, what? I do not understand how one can define environment using only the word life, for that it will be necessary to say, that scientists, researchers, and professionals define environment considering location, biological, chemical existence, functionality, vitality, effects, and consequences as some of the aspects with the major relevance of environment.

Besides all the groups mentioned before are the ancestors, tribes, and indigenous that refer to the environment regarding the connection that exists between the environment and all life in the world, not only in the spiritual sense, and the capacity to survive the seasons and world transformations through time, but also the loss of those sensitivities and how it will be possible to reconnect and recover the connection human beings – environment – life. The earth, land, air, and water, are a minimal part of all the environments that exist in the world, and important, indivisible part of the life of animals, plants, microorganisms, and every sense of life that exists and that is shared.

Looking carefully at both principal positions, it will be possible to see one common aspect in all the knowledge that was shared, and it was in all the research, publications, and studies is "life", which is the most practical, simple, common, and less scientific way to see the environment and even compare environment with life is through making an exercise of comparison.

It is common to see how it has increased the wrong idea on how the negative impact on the environment only affects the near areas where occur these specific events without considering it not only affects that area, when in reality affects the whole world, diverse actions, events, institutions, organizations, and even positions have been born to know, understand, defend and protect the environment, but the number of challenges to surpass are major than their capacity.

The environment is a world inside the world, rich in mystery, history, and evolution capable of giving and protecting life, but also is continuously being damaged, and affected negatively, is capable of stopping protecting life and producing destruction and death not because is the intentions or purpose of the environment but because the actions and omissions of human being against the environment.

- ✓ Is now when the environment is important?
- ✓ Why is it now that human beings need to worry about the environment?

No, the environment always has been important, is not now when humans need to worry about the environment it has always been important, it always that human beings need to worry about the environment, but now when every most visible damage that humans have caused to the environment, is now when the level of indifference to the environment is higher, a situation that makes it necessary, and indispensable to increase the number of actions, activities, to protect the environment. The environment with his/her secrets has not only given life but also inspired love and shared secrets to evolution, to produce the advancements, the security that have today.

From the beginning of history even before it was the first recorded, follows, studies of the environment, and the different advancements known today the environment have provided all the necessities and facilities that human beings and all living beings in the world require for subsistence. The environment has demonstrated to be a source of life and energy from which human beings also is the source for all these exigencies and necessities, even when the environment is rich in energy and it also is being exploited without hesitations and responsibilities, the history of the studies, and research that many scientists and professionals have carried on are integrated by diverse elements, some of which have been capable of identifying through time, but there are others that even today with the technological advancements haven't been capable to identify and/or understand.

Is time to stop only thinking that the environment is different in every place or location of the world and it represents an obstacle in taking care of the environment, is time to demonstrate how the environment is also different in the same place, and is always changing and transforming, so if the environment is always moving, changing, suffering transformations how it will capable to study or even to use the energy that the environment is capable to provide.

If the environment is always in constant movement how is capable of suffering the consequences of climate change? Even when the environment is in constant transformation, the effects of factors that produce contaminations, technology advancements, and the complement of society, exigencies are capable of reaching and affecting the environment no matter their movement or change, and location.

Dolefully is necessary to mention two examples where the environment has changed drastically due to the actions of human beings and that even when the past years there is a great percentage of danger and damage caused, and even with those damages caused to the environment it doesn't stop, and don't give up, every day continue given lessons and surprises, demonstrating that the environment is a very challenging homework to everyone, even to scientist, researchers, professionals from the past a, present, and future, and is even more challenging for those that are continuously trying to explain the importance and necessity of protect the environment, as well some of the many and diverse surprises that the environment is capable of give can be mentioned the land, tress, rivers, near Chernobyl has started to give sign of life, even when the amount of radiation still be very dangerous for life, during the last few years it has been observed to observe the returning, and surviving of certain animals, and reborn of plants and mushrooms which has created a numerous of questions between scientific being in some cases questions related to the mutations, and changes of the biological and chemical body of plants, the returning or seen of animals, as well as the mysterious of the environment, but more important is a call of attention, because so it pass many years without any sign of life or possibilities of recover it has also shown than when it starts recovering it is completely different and unknown, as how it was known and registered.

Another sad example of how the environment negatively shifts and affects the world is the event that occurred with the nuclear plant Fukushima which also has created changes, and produced an important impact on the environment, especially on ocean life, these two examples were capable of seeing how the actions of human beings cause damage to the environment to a great extension and it has affected the world on different levels being the most affected the area that is close or directly affected, and the area that is far or not even near it was also affected in less percentage but it was affected.

An interesting example of environment changes is encountered in Africa where due to different types of conditions are places with such extreme change where the level of drought is extremely high affecting and causing deaths of all life (rivers, plants, animals, agriculture, and humans), at this point all the changes of the environment can be seen negative changes, and there is where come up the surprises, no not all the environment changes are negative, is what the observation of the environment changes that emerge more questions, incertitude, and doubts. In this example, exists a complex situation where the human being's actions and omissions are present as well is also present the natural temperatures and weather of Africa which made a combination of elements, complexity, and at the same time difficult understanding, and contribute to the transformations and reduction of the temperature and drought being one of the risks, and danger with a high level of complexity that suffer Africa and that carry on to the see and experience the existence of different situations, whereas a part of Africa suffers drought in a very high and/extreme level is another part of Africa the flood cause damages in levels that can surpass the normal level or amount in the same month in different years in which how the increased the levels and frequency of floods.

The creation of strategies, and mechanisms, capable of solving or transforming this challenging situation does not only correspond to scientific, governments, institutions, people, and society, it also depends on other aspects such as understanding the country, territory, and reconnecting, and re-establish the relation human beings and environment is with that combination of actors, knowledge and understanding that it will be possible to obtain a solution, a response to this challenge.

The tree wall is not only an idea or project it is a reality where it has been grown in Africa for the last few years and continues to be extended, growing, and maintained, it is important to mention the intervention and participation of people, institutions, organizations, and governments in this action, and how even with the challenges of African territories, weather, that tree wall is growing and being extended but not only have created the bases for the reborn of earth, and land transformations is also generating a change of the environment a new environment capable to protect not only animals, given birth to grown plants, and create a new life system. The Sahara Desert, known by the extension, and particularities as the sand, high and low temperatures, sand storms, and very little sign of water and plants, has created a great and uncountable number of theories, stories, and legends.

Unfortunately, on the other side, the majority of people do not know the diverse species of animals and plants that exist in the Sahara Desert as just like that the existence of water sources has encountered a new change where in recent years it has happened an interesting phenomenon that even when is not that never happens before, is now when the frequency with which it occurs has been increased as well as the amount or level of it.

- ✓ What are these events?

These events are more than rain, storms, and snow which have contributed to the presence of a change in the environment, the increasing possibilities of the existence of rivers, and lakes, in the desert, survival of plants, and animals, those changes have generated the question of:

- ✓ Which are profound changes that the amount of rain and snow it will produce in the present and future in the Sahara Desert?
- ✓ How the change in the Sahara Desert is going to affect the world?

Since is known one of the most interesting, complex, and difficult to understand is the capacity of movement of the environment for example the way how the Sahara Desert Dust is capable of traveling around the world transforming and helping to maintain the environment in all the world, event that occur during sand storms the sand of the Sahara Desert travels through the world.

- ✓ With those changes what will be changes in the Sahara Desert sand journey?

The other aspect that has been changing in the Sahara Desert is related to the sand storms, even though always been sand storms, and have traveled outside the Sahara Desert throughout the world is known that in actuality the frequency and amount of the sand and sand storms travel has changed.

- ✓ How those changes will impact the present and future?
- ✓ How the increments of rain and snow will impact the Sahara Desert sand storms?

Is not possible to forget the example of environmental change that is given by those countries that protect and try to continue protecting their environment allowing to increase their evolution without affecting or putting on risk the life of all living beings that are in the country and have a quasi-perfect harmony between human beings and the environment so far it was mentioned a few examples of how environment not only change, also it has been capable of generating intrigue, doubts, questions, and it has increased the curiosity and challenges and even more, it will be possible to describe the environment with all their particularities, interrogatives, and transformations (good and bad).

Today is common to listen to people refer to environment protection saying that only a few countries in Europe are the ones that look to protect the environment, due to their culture, education, location, government interest, size of the country situation where believe that is far from true, in the world besides the Europe countries are many countries in the world that try and to protect their environment, this battle to integrate and protect the environment is not easy and sometimes they have many challenges to surpass as being one of the economic factors that have more impact in national and international ambit, also being capable of generating difficulties, backward, and even retardment on the actions that those countries are and going to carry on to protect their environment.

The environment is not shared by two or more countries, is shared by all the world, an interesting consideration that it has been encountered is one where an important part of society from different countries says that only rich and developed countries are the ones that want, care, can and will protect the environment while that poor and no developed countries cannot, will or care about protecting the environment, situation that required to evaluate the weakness and the by which the society only think that the responsibility and obligation of protecting the environment only correspond to the government and them do not have nothing to do.

A situation that is not possible to leave outside a third and probably the more conflicted position is the one where the developed countries are the ones that have more influence, negative impact, and damage caused to the environment, and who don't have any type of interested on protecting the environment using as excuse the necessity of continue the advancements and comply with the society exigencies. As is seen those are only a few of the multiple positions that exist in the world referring to the environment and in which no doubt the most powerful positions that exist and can be encountered in all the sectors, as well the most common to listen:

- ✓ Is the government is the one that is responsible for the law and protecting the environment, not the people?

It can be used as an example to explain the delicate situation of the environment a coin has two sides or faces, in the case of the environment each face is represented one by understanding the environment, and the other side by challenges to not understanding and compromising with the environment, those two faces of the coin require not only effort but also required responds to a very long list of questions that all start with the same word "Why" and where the answer it will carry to individual and collective responsibilities.

The environment today is very different from how it was in the past and how it will be in the future, the changes and transformations of the environment are closely related to the actions of human beings, who use them as an excuse for the accomplishment of society exigencies, the advancements, and even the world transformations, but those actions and omissions generating no positive changes in the environment, by the contrary it has produced negatives impact and situations of risk accompanied with the rise of events that are and can be dangerous and uncontrollable for all living beings in the world, as a result of the actions and missions of human beings the environment is making a call of attention to make not only changes but also adaptations and consider strategies and mechanisms that help to protect the environment and comply with the world and society exigencies.

The environment is a call of attention, to see the damage, risks, and danger that all living beings are suffering in the present, as the unprecedented events that occur in the present and can continue happening in the future or can be more dangerous, and cause more damage that can be thought or considered, is also being forgetting the aspect of with all the negative actions, and omissions.

- ✓ How is going to respond to the environment?

Doing this is one of the most important and difficult questions that every human being has to respond to, producing as result that the answer results can be simple and complex at the same time, beside the answer that can be given, is required to consider that the question also shows the existence of an evasive attitude to respond and admit responsibilities, as well it also demonstrates the most evasive attitude and the most number of no response as fear, lack of knowledge, insecurity, disinterest, and feelings of disconnection. This is not the only question that humans need to respond to the environment and is not the only to respond to questions is also to carry those responses to actions.

Each and every one of the lives that integrate the environment also work separately but they also depend on each other to act, comply with their functions, and responsibilities, protect, and give life because only by working as a team they can function, as equal as the from the action and life of human being which carry on activities individually, and as a team. A wrong belief is that the environment not only is a source of commodities, and forgetting that, is also an important source of security, life, knowledge, beauty, share of peace, and love for all the living beings in the world, as equal, what makes that the obtention of knowledge from the environment is one of the biggest challenges that human beings face from the past, present and future.

The environment is integrated by a combination of elements, life, systems, organisms, and microorganisms that make it rich, special, unique, and in constant movement, and transformation where each one of them has its challenges, even when they all suffer negative consequences that go on the different speeds, events, and situations, resulting in contradictions and carrying them to take into consideration how the environment is capable of working together as a team, and at the same time they are different, from each one, and have they one particularity.

A wrong belief is that environment protection and the implementations for the protection of the environment can wait and can be postponed due is not primordial or is not urgent contrary to that is what the reality and day-by-day events show and demonstrate, and is that the environment no needs or can't continue to wait for a specific hour, day, or week, month, or year to take actions and implement strategies to the reduce and/or eliminate the damage, danger, and negative impact that it has, and is caused to the environment change because every minute, every hour is changing, and those changes are being increased more rapidly as equal to the consequences produced by the different actions and omissions that human beings do.

Relation to Human Beings and Environment

The relation between human beings and the environment has existed since the origin of the world and history, it has always been part of each other protecting each other, surviving, and surpassing the challenges together, as a consequence of that relation it is possible to say that life it has been capable to continue advancing, changing, adapting, and suffering transformations until what is today, and it will continue changing in the future.

Environment and human beings have suffered transformations, and evolutions with time, but also for a long time existed until the human being necessities of advancements, ambition, change of lifestyle, the number of exigencies of human beings, start increasing and the relation between environment-human beings begin to be lost, given origin a to the process of separation, forgot, loss of the connection whit the environment and life, making that human beings change their path and start the process of the environment destruction.

Today when studying the environment on any professional or not professional ambit it will be possible to find multiple definitions and explanations regarding the meaning of environment which have been presented in different ways, sectors, and levels, from the house to the first school's studies level, until reaches society, professionals, international organizations, and government all of those definitions and explanations present the environment only as a source of energy and source of materials to satisfy society's necessities and exigencies making today that it has more mention as the negative effects of climate change, how leaving outside the real relation between environment – human beings can be understood or know what is the environment.

- ✓ Why is important?
- ✓ What is the meaning of the relation between the environment, and human beings?
- ✓ How many discussions, conversations, and studies, exist regarding the relation environment – human beings?
- ✓ Why do I have to do something?

A very common and simple answer to those questions is I don't know, I didn't know about the existence of a relation between human beings and the environment, let others do something, I always, sometimes, frequently do something to protect the environment but they do not, questions, disgust, anger, and contradictory feelings, are part of the relation human beings and the environment, but those are not the only questions there many other questions, to which the answers it demonstrates the existence of different feelings, contradictions and disappoint, as also the perception of failure and incapacity to comply with the goals.

- ✓ Since when and how has the relation between Human Beings and the Environment?

An answer that can contribute and help to understand the question and different answers, positions, and points of view is the one that says that could be since life exists, or the answer referred to the relation between human beings and the environment exists from the moment of born, and the natural essence reached so difficult, challenging, commercial, and even related to exploitation.

Understanding the relation human beings – and the environment can be difficult, complex, and contradictory, even for some groups impossible, which it is considered indispensable to examine this relation the use of a coin as an example, where each side of the coin represents one side of the environment, and the other side the human beings.

From the side of the coin that represents the environment it will be seen that since the beginning of times, human beings have depended on and used the environment to live and surpass the many challenges of their life through time such as the change of season, temperatures, and even the obtention of food, a place as it can be protected from rain, breeze, storms, high and low temperatures, the environment has provided to human being what they need without asking anything in return, through the time, the environment provides to human being knowledge and capacity to understand and share the changes, and transformations of the environment from which human being has been capable to see and know the changes of the environment, microorganisms, animals, plants and the difference environment elements even when there are much that still be a mystery.

On the other side of the coin are the human beings who during a time in the past it was capable of living in harmony with the environment causing no damage, but it did not pass much time when human beings started losing that connection, that relation that has with the environment with only one idea “progress, a satisfaction of lifestyle” without any limitations, and not any measures which that have been increasing the negative impacts, and consequences until the levels that have today, as also the loss of an important number, and percentage of the environment, species that are important and indispensable for the life of all living being in the world.

The existence of harmony between human beings and the environment doesn’t mean that human beings must sacrifice, or give up those commodities, security, and protection, it means to make, a change, and adapt and continue maintaining and having all those things but with the connection, re-connection, peace, and life of all living beings for the present and future.

- ✓ How does a relation that has existed since the beginning of life between the environment and human beings get lost and transformed with the only idea of satisfaction, economic benefit, and exploitation?

It is possible to say that the connection between the environment and human beings has been unequal at all levels for a long time since the past reached the present, and even despite the effort that is being made by a small group of people, institutions, and organizations, who have to surpass the differences and challenges in the relation human beings and the environment are major than the positive results, and far from a positive relation.

Today is not only important but also indispensable to evaluate, and consider those aspects, and events that have damaged, and affected negatively the relation the environment and human beings, see where it has failed, and how it is possible to repair the damage caused by that relationship in today's world. How it will be possible to create a good, successful, and durable on-time relations environment – human beings where there is a legitimate connection to the environment, sensitivity, and a feeling of protection and no damage, where harmony is the principal base of this relation?

Past, present, and future of the relation human being – environment will always have challenges due to the particularities, changes, and transformations that each one (human being, and environment) suffer every day, at different velocities and levels.

- ✓ What makes this relation ample, complex, and not static?

Authors, researchers, scientists, lawyers, and jurists have positions from which it is possible to refer to three groups that sometimes can share ideas, and positions, also enter into contradictions with no agreements between each other, and in others can give origin to the creation of disputes and contradictions, the first group says that it doesn't exist any relations between human beings and environment, the second group says that there exists and always exists in relation to human beings- environment, the third group a position that says that the relation between human beings and the environment, and the fourth group says that the relation between human beings and the environment only exist to the environment provide what human being need all those groups and positions consider diverse aspects and interest forgetting an important aspect which is that the human being and environment as separate have each one of the differences where the human being is not capable to reach to a minimum of possibilities without the environment concerning the environment the death of all living beings it will increase, but working as a team as one human being and environment will be capable to surpass and provide life, survive and surpass challenges.

Taking some of the most important, everyday, and common aspects that distinguish the life of human beings and the environment then it will be able to see that there are not only similarities, they are equal situations, events, and characteristics in both the environment and human being even much more than differences which produce as consequences how human beings have lost the perspective and direction on seeing how the life and the spread of all the activities, and actions for the survival of human beings are linked to the environment and are not separated from each other. Some of the characteristics, events, and situations that the Environment and Human Beings share are mentioned in a continuation:

Not Static, the environment and human beings are not statics are in constant movement, the accomplishment with actions, and activities every minute, every second, demonstrating the importance, necessity, and indivisible of the relation of life with movement, human beings are not separate of life and environment an example, even when it believes or think that trees are statics because it grows and keep the roots in the same place, it has been shown and proved that by the contrary of that, trees have their own movement even when in the occasion is not perceived or seen by human beings.

Always changing, change is one the more complex characteristics that share human beings and the environment since the change in the environment and the change on the human being is the results of actions of human beings actions, and omissions, is due to those actions of human beings produce impacts on the environment that generate changes on it, and those changes produce negative consequences on human beings creating the necessity of increase the actions, strategies, and mechanisms to reduce and stop negative effects that affect life and survival of all living beings in the world.

Adaptations, actions, and activities are tight to the world changes, globalization, internationalization, and integrations have originated the necessity for all life to adapt to those transformations that come over time (past, present, and future) showing that always is necessary to adapt to new events, situations, circumstances, and challenges that must be completed by taken decisions and considering all life, all sectors, all ambits.

An important aspect that is important to not forget is that human beings are only one part of the biggest and most complex system of life that is shared with the environment, animals, and plants, human beings, and all life never forget that are not capable of surviving alone, and their adaptation depends of the environment, animals, and plants, all life capacity of adaptation.

Biological, and chemical body changes, as equal the human beings body has different biological and chemical compositions and acts differently in every human being, generating different consequences also the environment, animals, plants, and all life have different biological and chemical body compositions and also suffer different types and levels of changes, and consequences suffering in both cases that can be referred as a natural process or events, and as consequences of the actions and/or omissions are not different, and it is not possible to say that the consequences that both suffer, suffering, damage, sickness, death, and the capacity for survival is only one of the aspects that are produced as a result of the biological and chemical body compositions and are only a few aspects that have created the born of curiosity and necessity to carry on research, studies, and strategies by scientists, doctors, lawyers, jurists, researchers around the world.

Legislation and Environment

The first thing that people think or relate to when referrer to legislation is punishment as a consequence of an activity or action that has been committed against the law, human beings, and all life, but is not related to prevention, protection, and even less with the environment, which in many cases is considered as less important or with nonrelevance, causing the existence of conflicts, contradictions, discussions and debates in all level and sectors, but also it has demonstrated the existence of an important level of lack of knowledge of the importance and necessity of the Environment protection and the existence of the environment legislation (national and/or international).

Since the origin of law and legislation in the world researchers, professionals, and specialists have as one of their principal objectives the study and explanation of the meaning, evolution, and importance of the legislation in general and for the specific area of study and development for which it has been generated the necessity of study.

In a general way legislation is the rules, and legal norms that were created to provide protection, and security to all living beings inside a territory and/or country through obligations, responsibilities, and sanctions, but over time, and transformations it gives origin to the existence of international legislation's what gives results the existence and obligatory complement of national and international legislation's being one of the most important subject the Environment which though those legislations it has left clear that the protection of the environment is an obligation by equal to all the countries, to all human being in the world.

Even when the legislation has a long history and has been subject to reforms, derogations, creation, and approval of new legislation that goes according to the new and changing exigencies of the society and for the protection of all living beings, but unfortunately is necessary to say that the legislation it has not be able to comply completely with the protection of all living beings and specifically with the protection of the

Environment has failed being as well not capable of comply with their objectives with success and efficiency, and efficacy.

Another aspect that has influenced the lack of success of the legislation's is the not existence of enough legislations and agreements, and implemented on time, due to the creation, discussion, approval, and implementation of environment legislation and the damage and negative impact that is suffering the environment has an important difference on time that reduce the possibility of efficacy, efficiency, effectiveness, and success.

Unfortunately, a sad situation that it results impossible to deny or stop is the one that refers to how human beings have lost the connection and interest in the environment as well for the protection of the environment originating that that human beings not always tried to protect the environment, and have redacted, discussed, and approved legislation's regarding the environment, on the contrary is necessary to remark that the legislation that today exists related to the environment have their origin in a recent data, making possible to see how in the last few years the existence of national and international environment legislation have suffered a very small increment, the existence of reforms, obligations, and correct implementation of environment legislation's through all the different countries in the world, without making any distinction, but also it has demonstrated the existence of an important number of challenges that still need to surpass, and showing the necessity of counter with the strategies and mechanisms that be capable to beat those challenges, and be applicable and durable in time, as going together with the changes of the world.

The environment not only request, but also demands a change on the legislation's, making that be time for a change in the environment legislation's process and time, always having present that the environment it does not stop suffering and being subject of damage as consequence of the wrong and/or illegal actions, and omissions that are capable of generating graves situation and increment of risks for the environment and life, due to those aspects together with other aspects and situations have contributed to increase one of the biggest challenge of the legislation's which is not other that the slow velocity on how the environment legislation's are being react to environment producing as results that for when the legislation has been approved it becomes another point that perhaps represents the most difficult, and complex aspect of the legislation's, as a consequence of the delay and time that the countries and international organizations take to carry on the study discussion, approve, and implement the legislation is extremely slow and negative, making it became obsolete and late by when is going to come into effect, and being necessary to those legislation's be subject of review and reform.

As well as the time represent one of the biggest and major problem in relation to the legislation and the environment, in contradictions to that situation is possible to mention the existence of important legislation's that showed their relevance and permanence through time as is the case of Montreal Protocol (1997), UN Framework Convention on Climate Change (1992), Kyoto Protocol (1997), Paris Agreement (2016), Convention on Biological Diversity (1993), Cartagena Protocol on Biosafety (2003), Convention International Trade in Endangered Species (CITES) (1973), Convention on the Conservation of Migratory Species of Wild Animals (1979), Conventions to Combat Desertification (1994), Ramsar Westlands Convention (1971), UNESCO World Heritage Convention (1972), Law of the Sea (1982), Straddling Fish Stocks Agreements (2001), Basel Convention on Hazourds Wast (1992), Stockholm Convention on POPs (2004), Rotterdam Convention on PIC (2004), and the Miumala Convention Mercury (2013) in addition that the countries have approved diverse legislations, despite the challenges meaning that it is growing interest in this subject, but:

- ✓ How is going to be the implementation?
- ✓ How and who is following and assuring the fulfillment and success of those legislations at the national and international levels?

Nevertheless when and the number of countries that sign the conventions, agreements, protocols, and legislations they face an important backward and challenge when it refers to the implementation, application, and complement of their objectives and goals, since it has been demonstrated that is not capable to reach to the level of complement, success, that is was expected, on contrary it has shown to get complete participation and involvement of the countries that have signed and ratified those legal instruments to protect the environment, where in many cases and situations the lack of interests and actions it has become the great allied of the failure in the environment protection. Is not only to sign, and approve legislation is also to comply with the objectives, principles, and supervision of the obligations and responsibilities as well as the imposition of a sanction for those who do not comply with the obligations and responsibilities established on those legislations and be capable of creating and implement strategies, mechanisms to solve the possible problems and challenges than can occur in the present and future.

The fulfillment of the national and international legislations does not depend on the governments alone, it also depends on the actions that every human being does explaining and being capable to reach to the people on how the omissions that they do, develop, and maintain it also a great contributor to damage and put in danger the environment and life, and every omission that every human being/person stops or left to do or just doesn't do, it have reach the time when is extremely necessary, and is an environment exigency to human beings to understand that the only existence, of national and international environment legislations is not enough to protect the environment, is not going to work and produce results expected and protect the environment reducing the level of damage and danger by just saying there is a law for that, or is the government, and international authorities, national and international organizations, institution, and NGOs who have to comply with the legislations, guarantee the obedience, compliment, and imposition of the sanctions established on the legislations, agreements, and conventions,

National and International Environment Legislations were born not only to create a law, but also to comply with the requirement, or to say there is an environment law, agreements, protocols, and conventions, born with a purpose, by a necessity, and a reality, which is the protection the environment and all life, if the environment is not protected, producing as a consequence that the life is not protected, if the environment is not protected then damage, danger, and death it will increase and cover the world without any distinction of country and/or political, economic or social position. The responsibility and obligation to comply with the national and international environment legislations do not require to be asked:

- ✓ Why is important to comply with national and international environment legislations?
- ✓ Does it is necessary to comply with the agreements, protocols, and conventions?
- ✓ Is necessary, important, and/or relevant to comply with the national and international

environment legislations, agreements, conventions, and protocols?

- ✓ Why it is important for people and/or society in general to comply, help, and contribute to the fulfillment, and success of the national and international environment legislations as well as with the agreements, conventions, and protocols?

It also requires compliance by government, scientific, business, or legal professionals and not professionals from all the sectors are not referred to the society alone, is not directed to a specific sector or group, is directed to all human beings without taking and/or making any distinguish on the age, countries, religion, economic level every with the same responsibility, the same obligation, and it will suffer the same sanction.

In actuality exists discussions, debates, and diverse positions in favor and against regarding the implementation or not of the national and international environmental legislations, in occasions it is possible to see actions and protests carried on by climate change and environment activists and protest where their actions are against the real sense of environment protection and compliment of the legal norms and legislations, being destructive and damaging even when it shows a contrast of feelings, in which it has become a frequent response or justification for that actions the failure and no compliment of the national and international environment legislation originating a series of questions, and questioning about the existence and effectiveness of the national and international environment legislations as well as the agreements, conventions, and protocols and their lack and weakness on the obligatory accomplishment and capacity of the imposition of sanctions, one of the questions and/or questioning that have an impact in the world is:

- ✓ Are the national and international environment legislations responsible for those actions?

This should not be seen only as questions or questioning, or even as a weakness of the national and/or international legislations, agreements, conventions, and protocols on the contrary it must be considered as a wake-up call that the national and international environmental legislation is falling and needs to pay attention to those situations and events of environment legislations, assure accompanied by those actions is the existence of national and international legislation information, which has been always one of the most important and constant weaknesses that until today hasn't been corrected, it is needed to increase and expand the information on the environment, and legislations ensure that be capable of reaches to the society using different strategies, mechanisms, and with and without the use of technology, so it will be possible to reach to all in the same level of equality and capacity, as well in a language that can be understandably and adopted by everyone without any type of distinction of language location, and friendly way to be understood, and accepted.

One of the aspects that is subject of discussions is the relation that exists between the national and international environment legislations and human being which is characterized for been complex and integrated with differences, and similarities that instead of being reduced or eliminated it has increased, and where is the human being who have a major number of challenge to surpass, and needs to be capable to accept, apply and comply with the responsibilities, obligations, actions and comply with the sanctions that are imposed as consequence of their actions and/or omissions established in the national and international environment legislations, another challenges that the environment legislations face and have to surpass in the national and international ambit, is related to the political and government compromise and responsibilities in the environment protection which can go in different directions with their plans of development or business in a national and/or international level, were business and development have major interest on political and/or government ambit over the environment.

In the review of the International Environment Legislations that has existed since 1971 until today, it is possible to see the difference in compromise and integration of the countries in the environment protection, situation that has been evident through the number of countries that sign the agreements, countries, protocols, and international legislations, and how not all the countries signed the international legislations, agreements, and conventions producing difficulties in the obtention of the expected and required results, the same situation is capable of seeing is a national level where each country has redacted, approved, signed, and enter it comes into effect, and be implemented the environment legislation, but is not accepted and applied by all the political, government and society sectors in an equal level of obligation, responsibility, and sanction, is not an easy task to obtain the acceptation and compliance of the environment legislation more than a task is an obligation and a urgent necessity that need to be fulfilled.

An interesting change of situation it has been happening during the last few years in where it has been transformed and increasing the participation and involvement of international organizations that in the last few years it has become more participative not only in discussions, research, and debates, but also in the protection of the environment through studies, courses, seminars, and in the redaction, approbation, sign, and implementation of legislations, regulations, jurisprudence, acts, conventions for the protection of the environment, also facing an important weakness in how to connect and diffuse the information about the environment legislations with the society, business, institutions, organizations, and government on how their work to comply with the objectives and reach the expected results, along with the international organizations it has born institutions, organizations, associations, groups, and NGOs that are trying to get involved and guarantee the success of the national and international legislations but in a very limited and reduced ambit of action, and possibilities, but unfortunately that effort to increase the participation and integration of all sectors in the environment protection through the participation, knowledge, discussions and diffusion of the national and international environment legislation, it doesn´t count with their objectives, as well is has showing to continue having important weakness that does not allow to reach all the society and sector on in a equal conditions.

It has been also observed how the national and international environment legislations have been increasing as long as the negative impact of climate change on the environment in the world increases to dangerous levels, having to confront new and unexpected challenges that the national and international legislations have to protect the environment, also the slowness and/or negative advancement and obtention of the results is directly related to the exigencies of the society to have commodities and facilities demonstrating that is capable to make human activities and lifestyle more comfortable, but:

- ✓ What is the price that the environment has to pay for human being's satisfaction?
- ✓ How will the national and international environmental legislations be capable of

acting and complying with the environment and society?

- ✓ How society will be capable of adopting and fulfilling national and international environmental legislations?
- ✓ Why is so important to know, manage, and put into practice the national and international environmental legislations?
- ✓ What difference it will make more diffusion of information regarding the national and international environmental legislations?
- ✓ How are going to respond to those questions?

Those are without doubt some of the many questions that are not only made to be capable of giving a simple and quick answer, is also to be able to produce and increase a reflection, on the attitude and actions of human beings concerning the environment, there is no simple or only response to those questions each question has multiple and complex answers that are capable of generating an important impact in life and the environment, locally and globally it will create a chain reaction that can be positive and/or negative according to the answer and the action taken, but also makes to think int the actions that are necessary to implement in order of guarantee the existence and permanence in time of the national and international environment legislations. Is time to stop thinking, and acting individually, and separately, is time that all the countries and sectors in the world start working as a team to protect the environment, the environment is the life in the world not only in one specific country and/or territory. count on global environmental legislation.

Now is the moment when all the countries in the world must have to count with a national environment legislation, incorporate, and implement the teamwork as indispensable as well as recognizing that the management and advancement that every country in which the concerning regarding this subject is disproportional, making it difficult for the countries to comply with the minimum requirements on legislations, number of environment legislations that is needed and in the existence and the functionality of institutions that are necessary to comply and make effective the dispositions, and legal norms of the environment legislations, faces problems not only in the government and political sector, but also in the lack of professionals, knowledge, preparedness, equipment, integrations, and communication, which makes that the amount of challenges increases into a high percentage, is no less true that legislation is not perfect and they are not mean static, needs to be capable of going in the same direction and velocity as the environment and society to provide protection to the environment.

Sadly is necessary to mention one of the biggest enemy of the environment and life that is not other than ¨fear¨ which in many cases it have gaining the battle the fear of proposing and/or discussing environmental legislation in the National Assembly, Parliament, Congress, or Chamber, thereby, any high-level government instance presenting as justification the reaction and impact on society, business, or economic sector is also one of the major enemies that the environment and life have to surpass and only will be capable to be surpassed with a joint of all sectors without any distinction or difference, recognition of gender equality to protect and work in favor of the environment, and the loss of fear.

- ✓ How it will be possible to win the battle against fear?

- ✓ How it will be possible to transform the fear into the courage to protect the environment and life?

Feelings, actions, and situations that require individual and collective evaluation, reflection, and consensus of the importance and grave situation through which the environment and all life and living beings in the world have to pass and surpass, and is not a maintain itself or transient situation that is going to be solved by itself if not that without the correct evaluation, intervention, and integration is going to continue, growing and getting more dangerous with the time.

Another big failure, and disadvantage of the national and international environment legislation's is referred to the capacity and ability to obey, and comply with the environment legislation, legal norms, and national and international conventions, as well as the incapacity of human beings' capacity of understand the consequences of affecting and/or invading, and/or modify the environment spaces, by all the sectors (governments, national and international organizations and institutions, economic, society) demonstrating that the knowledge, diffusion and obligation of compliment with the environment legislation is not being successful and is not reaching to everyone, producing as consequence the necessity and urgency of create, and implement new strategies as well as change and adapt those strategies and mechanisms that already exists always maintaining present that the environment legislations do not only look to protect the environment, but also is protecting the life of human beings, and all life in the world.

Development and Environment

One of the most controversial, complex, and delicate aspects that produce different types, and levels of effects on the environment is the development of a country and society, the compliance of the exigencies of society and the development of the country goes in a different direction creating a very dangerous situation for both (the environment and human being), increasing death, environment catastrophes, and disasters in all around the world which does not look if is a developed or not developed country, neither see the economic position of the human being the consequences are being suffered by everyone.

- ✓ How humanity has reached the point where the development of a country and the satisfaction of everyday society's exigencies for more modern, and actualized technology have become more important than life, more important than the survival of all life in the world?

- ✓ Since when does the development of a country or the necessities of society mean destruction, killing, death, and extinction?

It shouldn't development mean survival, protection, and union between the environment and human beings? where development should be working as a team with the environment, going in the same direction, not separately, is seen how many developed countries have provided better services, and life style for their people, but is failing in provide the correct protection to the environment, and countries that are not developed have more tools and sensitivity for the protection of the environment situation that have created a contradictory how two different situation due when more developed is the country more damage cause to the environment and less legislations, tools, strategies, mechanism have to protect the environment, when it should be contrary it doesn't matter the size, amount of population or location of the country there most share the same level of experience, capacity, and interest not only in the development of the country economy, and business, also should be directed into the protection of the environment in their country and around the world, an example that can be mentioned is when the countries that are not developed have redacted, approve and implemented legislations, strategies, and educated to their population into the importance of development, thereby, in the protection of the environments, even when the country economic, and business advancement is a challenge that make difficult to comply with all their obligations, and responsibilities in a national and international level, is known the importance of the environment protection.

Determination is another factor which to work on the development of the country, business, and environment, it is possible to comply with all of their goals and obtain success without affecting the environment at any level or grade, at this point it is necessary is important to consider not only the development and advances of the country's economy and business are also needed to evaluate strategies, and mechanisms that can be applied in a way that does not reduce the capacity of comply with the society advancement and education, by the contrary be capable of increase the involvement of society in the development, integration and protection of the environment as also increase an indivisible integration and be part of the activities and actions of human beings from the smallest to the ampler, and complex.

It has talked about the development of countries, economies, and businesses, what is the meaning of development for the environment? What does development mean? in simple words, development is the action in which a determined situation, project, or work suffers a process of transformation to advance in growth offering major and different opportunities, is also to understand development as the process by which a negative aspect or situation suffers a transformation into positive, that action also generates situations, and events that affect (directly and not directly) diverse sectors of life, is not focused in only one ambit, with a reduced and centered effects and/or consequences, even more:

- ✓ What is the meaning and relation between determination and development at every stage result of the development?

Education is one of the relevant, important, and fundamental rights that every human being has, and also one of the most controversial, challenging, unequal, and changing in every country, and educational system, due to not every person having the same capacity to get access to education and many cannot access to any type of education even when is one of the rights, that have more challenges need to surpass, in the past, present and future, but when is referred to environment education in all level of education a common and always present challenge is the possibility of knowing what is the environment.

Environment education is important at all levels of studies, and teaching from the simplest to the most complex environment with the management of different subjects also is necessary to establish and determine when and how are going to start those studies and explain the uses, and benefits that can be obtained from the environment to satisfy all the necessities and exigencies, is where is a fail of teaching the importance, necessity, obligation of protect and integration with the environment, as also teach the negative impact and consequences that causes harm to the environment.

In actuality, education and sharing knowledge of the environment, have been reduced to the more basic and common aspects leaving the most profound subjects of the environment it has been left to science and scientific areas, so there will be those who study, complete research, and propose strategies to continue advancing in development areas, also has become in a subject that has been reduced, and almost eliminated in every country and education system is the understanding, connection, love, and reconciliation with the environment.

- ✓ How it will be possible to change this situation and increase the teaching and understanding of the environment in the world education system?
- ✓ How it will be possible to integrate education into the environment and development at the same time without affecting the environment and development?
- ✓ How education can provide strategies and mechanisms to continue advancing in the development of different sectors while the environment is being protected?

Education must not come only from schools also has to come from the needs of society, government, institutions, business, and means from all the sectors at the same level capable of reaching everyone equally, the integration of all as educators is important and relevant to success in development and environment, changing the role from teacher-student to teacher-student – teacher since even when a teacher or professional in the area have a certain level of knowledge it can obtain knowledge from other people is not leaving outside the people that even when they aren't a teacher or have professionals studies that have important environment knowledge that teacher or other professionals or people related to environment do being capable of producing and interesting exchange of knowledge, and information as result of the unlimited chain reaching to everyone in everywhere.

Policy, subject of constant controversy and conflict with environment, society, legislations, education, determination, and even health, and how is possible that a subject with such importance is capable to be so controvert when the objective and fundament of a policy is to provide mechanisms that contribute to the development and the protection of environment, on diverse situations, events, and cases is possible to observe how certain policy can affect negatively the environment with the use of justification and allegations regarding the protection of the environment that is working according the national and/or international legislations to provide and comply with the exigencies of society and contribute to the country development all the and diverse areas, also using as allegation that it appear is the compliance with international agreements or conventions, but when those allegations are presented as they are going against other legislations, conventions, treaties that exists that are not being considered due the relation whit the environment it get necessary to consider and evaluate how it will be possible to assure that the environment policy have more relevance, notoriety, capacity of produce more obligations, responsibilities, and impose sanctions without reducing, but always maintaining the importance, relevance of the environment policy, legislations.

One of the challenges and difficulties that are related to environment policies is the no consideration as important, not being implemented because diverse sectors consider the environment pleading lack of relevance that the policy presents, due to the protection and continuation of development, globalization, internationalization, businesses, economies, and exchange of supply for production but not taking care and generation of consequences, damage and violations of policy and environment nationals and/or international legislations, and other situation that born regarding policy conflicts or no compliment of an environment policy it can produce a legal conflict where to get a solution it will be necessary the intervention of a court of justice to get involved to produce a satisfactory solution to the controversy.

Industries, a sectors that have an important influence in the development process and the conflict between development – environment- and life, due to the mechanisms, materials, and strategies used by the different types of industries no matter the size those industries are capable of affecting one or another way the environment increasing levels of contaminations, death, health problems and increasing the negative effects of climate change not allowing that the mechanisms, legislations, actions that are being carried on, and can comply with their objectives and the obtention of positive results, by contrary are become one of the greats generator of backward of all possible advancements, due to the negative of the industries to change their strategies or way of working with allegations as costs, time, change of efforts, machinery', and that change of their form of working will not contribute to the development of the industries, economy, and country, presenting them as a possible to not get involved in the effort of reducing the damages that cause and/or are capable of causing.

Contrary to what those industries recognize, an important number of industries allege there are or have started a process of changing the work, machinery, materials, and strategies to work in a way that they can continue obtaining economic growth, while also being capable of contributing in the protection of the environment as create new possibilities for a short, medium, and long time, but also creating a new perspective in relation to the meaning of industries, development, and environment, as are getting more integrated to the nationals and international legislations demonstrating that industries are not apart and are the enemy of the environment, that as well the society has exigencies, the world changes and experiences new challenges industries are also capable to change, adapt to those challenges and work as a team with the same direction, objectives, and goals, situation that make a difference in the beliefs of some industries regarding the possibilities of growth, advances in these industries are not slow and/or impossible contrary it shows their growth goes at the same or even at the fastest velocity than the industries that are against the change and keep working using tools, material dangerous for the environment and life, demonstrating in many cases in which industries that protect environment has shown an increase and grown more rapidly than was expected.

Technology, equal as the industries the technology is the sector with a great capacity to generate discussions, contradictions, and conflicts since technology has become a part almost indivisible of human being activities that go from the simplest to the most complex aspects, activities, and actions of life (social, and professional, private and public) but even when technology has provided and numerous and important advancement, contributions, and benefits to the different sectors and people life, also are capable of causing damage to the environment due to many factors that involve the creation, development, and function of technology on the different ambits as scientific, medicine, research, industries, business, transportation, communication, education, social activities, as it is possible to see technology is present in every area, in every activity capable of damage the environment and life is also present not matter to what type or level of damage are being referred.

- ✓ How is possible that technology can be so dangerous to the environment and life at the same time that has produced significant advancement, helps research in different areas, medicine, and science, and contributes to diverse areas of professional and personal life?

Regarding these questions, there exist diverse positions the first position says that it looks to be a contradiction, and the second position sustains that technology is the only significance of advancement capable of producing positive results without causing damage at any moment, nevertheless, the positions mentioned is necessary to highlight that the assurance of no damage caused by technology is not being seen even regarding the materials, elements, and process of elaboration of the technology and how those materials are capable of producing a negative impact on environment and life, as also is contributing to the negative impact of climate change.

Technology, as well as other aspects mentioned, needs to be capable of adapting and working together to protect the environment and life and not to prejudice the environment and life under the offer under the image of being the great salvation of humanity and a great generator of advancement and development when in the behind is producing an increment of damage, destruction, death on the environment, animal, plants, human being into all life in the world. How technology will be capable of being part of the developments without affecting the environment and all living beings in the world? It should be the principal and first question of technology.

Resistance, is the development aspect with a majority of presence in every area, every ambit that can be found or mentioned as political economic, social, educational, business, industries, scientific, research, even between the environment groups, and environment activists who are an active part in this factor of development but also are present in the damage caused to the environment (directly and/or not directly, intentionally and/or not intentionally) it doesn't matter to what group is referred or the development process industries or even countries sectors it also needs to be integrated to the environment in the way that can continue with the development but without affecting the environment the protection of the environment and life of all living being in the world.

Resistance to change, adapt, and accept is present in every sector without any type of distinction, this resistance exists in many cases because of money gaining, fear, commodities, lack of knowledge, capacity, facility, and even time, which are related to which are on the contrary side of health, environment, life, protection, legislation, safe development, and even time, at this last point "time" it appears in all the different group that demonstrates resistance (resistance of adapting, resistance of change) as if time is a competition to win a prize without taking into consideration that is who manage the rules as the effects, consequences, results, damages or benefits in every instance and level of developments.

- ✓ Why resistance is present in those aspects who care about the protection of the environment and who do not have any interest in the environment?
- ✓ How resistance can be a great generator of conflict causing more damage?
- ✓ How it would be possible to transform those challenging aspects of resistance into strategies that can be applied to protect the

environment and all living beings in the world?

After reading those questions is no doubt that can be a challenge to combine all those strategies, mechanisms, and change of material, way to work, and all the elements that are born to the resistance into adaptation, incorporation, and integration into the same direction without letting the resistance elements will be capable to interfere in the protection of environment and live and become a part of it.

Resistance contains negative elements that even when it has been used and demonstrated as an important part of development, and progress produce a major level of damage and increase the impossibility of the obtention of positive results generating conflicts with legislation and even with development and producing backward in the economy, business, and industries advancements, reducing the possibilities of adaptations and creations into a new option, situations, events and transformations as resistance have negative elements but also contains positive elements that create a balance with the negative elements which is necessary to be capable of determining the correct level of economic balance and a way to transform the resistance not producing a disbalance between negative and positive resistance.

Business is a sector that involves small, medium, and big sizes of business, as also national and international, public and private, government, countries, and states, in which the influence and importance of business in the development of the economic sector and the country involve not only the internal (national) advancements but also in the international level. Business is capable of producing an important influence in the world even when not all businesses manage the economy at the same level or have that influence over the economy, their surroundings, and/or the survival and development of the country, at this point emerges the question:

- ✓ How business is capable of producing a negative impact on the environment?

Even when different types, sizes, or capacities of businesses are all responsible for the impact on the Environment, where they are working for development, that development that business is looking for is capable of generating damages on the Environment, which occurs because as all actions and activities in life, business is a large and no ending chain where every of the chain eye represents an action, event, a situation that their result in affects the Environment.

Business development doesn't escape having responsibilities, obligations, and even sanctions, it doesn't matter the type of business, the size or importance of the business, or the country of origin of the business their business development has to comply with national and international legislation internationals, agreements, being one aspect that business never taken into consideration it doesn't means that can't exist and continue growing and business must not forget that development process is necessary to survive and for survive needs to exists life, and life depends on the Environment survival and life.

In the present exists diverse ways (direct and not direct) in how Business impacts on Environment, and multiple ways how Business can continue being an important source of development without affecting the Environment, the interesting and more intriguing situation is how to create and implement the correct strategies and mechanisms that can comply with success the objectives of development and environment protection. Business development in actuality depends on a great percentage of technology, and without technology businesses, it will face important problems and challenges.

- ✓ What alternatives do businesses have to integrate development and the Environment?

Think in Business development involves other factors such as knowledge, people, professionals, not professionals that are part of business, locations, tools, machinery, community integration, recognition, acceptance, and knowing that failure of one of them means backward or slowness in Business development, but must not in the environment protection, this could be contradictory since a logical belief is that is business development got backward and/or slow it will also slow the way in how business it will protect the environment, but the reality is that is not, because even when both are depending of business they have different characteristics, elements, and are separate in the point that business development cannot stop or divert the environment protection.

Country, the country's development depends on all the national sectors as equal in their international integrations, to the world changes, society exigencies, and the government's actions to adapt and implement the mechanisms necessary to be part of and increase the development process and comply with the exigencies and requirements by the people of the country, environment, and all living being. Today is very common to see how more countries have changed their goals and directions of development and environmental protection not only with the same priority or intention but also at the same velocity, a contradictory situation is seen when countries are closing themselves and rejecting development in areas as education, professional integration, environment protection, instead of incorporating their countries as common areas allowing integration and teamwork, they are restricting them and closing important aspects of development creating backward, barriers, even when they call themselves open and hold the hand of development and progress, but today when globalization, technology, internationalization, and integration are in the first place of every ambit, even in every legislation of the world, countries actions demonstrate something different.

Is true that every country has different characteristics, have its particularities, but also is not less true that all countries share problems, and consequences of the actions that affect directly, and not directly the countries' developments, lives, and environment which means backward not only in development but also in time since development is not going on the same velocity on all the sectors (economics, social, educational, politics, professionals) producing as a consequence that even when the country show progress and develop in certain areas it have important problems in other areas as is the case of the Environment protection which is the most important weakness that every country share.

- ✓ How it the countries it will be able to advance and develop in the internal (national) sectors as well as in the protection of the environment separately when the environment impacts all living beings equally?

The countries have suffered changes on different ambits with also different capacities of managing those situations, some of those changes are produced by the existence of conflicts regarding territories and/or frontiers, which had a long history of existence, and today situations are others that carried to a lack or slow motion in the development process no matter the area of development on which the country is working on, it also creates diverse levels of challenges that required to surpass for the obtention of the expected results and success.

Technology and the Integration and Protection of the Environment

Technology is not from recent data, in point of fact it has a long trajectory, since the beginning of technology until today it has suffered multiple changes, and transformations, always maintaining the same direction continuing on the creation of new, different, and advanced technology, mechanisms, and it this ideas always has been presented as the great friend and saver of humanity and human being, but never it has been seen and presented the other side of technology, he side that effect the environment, the increase the separation of the integration and connection with the environment, the damage and increase of danger to the environment.

Why is important and/or necessary to evaluate, review, and determine a relation between environment and technology? The creation and development of technology are related to all of the life ambits but also is linked to the environment since to technology can function it requires the environment's resources, capacity, and wisdom, to be capable of reaching what human beings have caused damage, danger, and increased the level of risk, as, the destruction of big extensions of land for the installations of industries, production and different types of plants, and even places for the creation and development structures for space exploration but never with a limitation to observe the transformations that are being caused to the environment and life.

Since the origin of technology and its advancement the development of technology means an important and high level of destruction, contamination, and damage to the environment being on the contrary side of the protection of the environment, the material, locations, and bases, that are used for the development of technology does not limit or are changing the mechanisms, materials, strategies that use to comply with their obligations and responsibilities with the environment, life, nationals, and international legislations.

The relation that exists between environment and technology originates a series of questions as well it gives born to different groups each one has its particular and own point of view, it also produces discussions, debates, and even new points of view regarding the influence and impact of technology in the integration and protection of the environment, it will be possible to mention as a first group who sustain that technology and environment does not have any relation, the second group who said that it those exist a relation between environment and technology, the third group who consider themselves as neutral or just say they do not understand, and for that they will not get involved, the fourth group who say that technology it does harm, damage and cause danger to the environment, and a fifth group who say that technology does not cause any harm, damage and cause danger to the environment, but:

- ✓ It exists a common point between all of those groups?
- ✓ Is it possible to reunite and join all those groups in the same direction, with the same objective of environment protection?

In the last few years, it has been developed important and diverse advancements and promotions of Artificial Intelligence but as in every technology area and development, Artificial Intelligence is not perfect. Even when the development of any type of Artificial Intelligence it also means, represents, and shows the number of important damage and dangers to the environment, and life around the world, emerging as a consequence of the following question:

- ✓ How it be possible to technology continue advancing and developing its important tools without affecting and damaging the environment?

With all the promotion and publicity AI has received it has been forgotten that technology and AI cannot manage, and perceive all the situations, and events, and apply all the actions that life requires, and are necessities. No doubt cannot be done without the participation of human beings and that corresponds to the understanding, integrating, and understanding how to protect the environment no matter how advanced or good the technology, another undeniable aspect that has been forgotten and not taken into consideration is not only that without life is no technology, and while damage is caused to the environment, more increases the danger and more difficulties and challenges it will face the technology development.

Technology is a sector of human being's development that demonstrated to have two different faces one positive and one negative and that can result in contradiction, in one face shows to have an important negative impact on the environment, but is also capable of providing tools, and mechanisms to surpass some of the many challenges that exist regarding the integration and protection of the environment, but with the complexity and constant changes of technology is necessary and obligatory to identify, determine and establish the different technology tools capable of providing help and which by contrary it will produce and increase the damage to the environment, for example, much are asking about the Artificial Intelligence:

- ✓ Artificial Intelligence can contribute in some aspects but is it a good tool that protects the environment or on the contrary, it will create more damage?

Is important not to incur the aspect of thinking about the help and facilities that Artificial Intelligence produces for human beings with the effects that AI produces on the environment which are two very different situations, ambits, and aspects.

As with every sector technology doesn't escape challenges, and difficulties, as well it shows once more its dependence on the environment's survival and the changes of the environment, an example of that can be mentioned in the communications which are sustained by the existence of technology but what happened with constant changes of the environment, weather pattern, and situations of risk or danger, in that case, the communication is susceptible to fail living people, communities, cities, country or even the world without communications, as how it could be possible to see is a chain where it demonstrates that while more danger and damage is caused to the environment more damage, risk and danger suffer all living beings in the world.

- ✓ What is the means of technology?
- ✓ Which is the true reason for which technology exists?
- ✓ What is being looked at with the technology?

The answer could be simple as the first answer it will come is to facilitate life, to create commodities, to provide protection, and a better way of survival, but is necessary to think and consider if it has been so on an equal level to all human beings in the world and for the environment or only has been developed for specific sectors o levels of people and have also forgotten about the protection that environment needs.

The Environment has particular, unique, and special characteristics that make it require constant monitoring, and vigilance to be able to know and detect the changes, and negative effects suffered by the Environment despite the great advances that Artificial Intelligence has achieved, it is not possible to determine its capacity and effectiveness in the protection of the Environment.

Much has been said that the protection of the environment depends on all sectors, not only on a specific group or sector, to which the possibility of including Artificial Intelligence has been considered, which cannot function and act independently and individually from human beings, it is also important to mention that even when artificial intelligence can be employed or used for the protection of the environment its functions and activities will be limited and it will not be able to effectively comply with all the aspects that are necessary and required, many are the limitations that are present.

One of the challenges of Artificial Intelligence in the Environment lies in the particularities and differences that exist in Artificial Intelligence and the Environment, but also in how to transform the disadvantages and challenges of Artificial Intelligence into factors that can be of help without affecting the Environment and advances in technology.

Climate Change and Environment

Climate Change is a term that was adopted in recent years to refer to the changes that the world regarding the climate for long periods, but also to the weather changes in a short period since in every season, every day is possible to feel and appreciate how the world is suffering dramatics changes, transformations, which on contrary to be positive are increasing the negative impacts, the negative effects in all the areas, and ambits of life affecting all living being in the world, different positions exists about climate change.

The terminology Climate Change reunites in only one term all the changes that the world suffers in terms of global warming and global cooling always working separately and not reaching a common agreement but both events have occurred in the past, and one of the points of discussions and disagreement is the possibility that as how global warming can happen and/or is happening also the global cooling can occur where in both positions their have denials of the possibilities that can occur due the actual conditions and changes of society and world, differences has, are occurring around global warming and global cooling, and always it will be existing different positions, opinions, and ideas, and those positions it also is around the today know climate change.

Recognition of the existence of climate change, integrated by scientists, society, lawyers, professionals, international organizations, institutions, and NGOs who through their studies, and evidence, agree in the existence of climate change and the effects and changes on the effects those groups, do not deny that climate change has always existed, but they also recognize that the characteristics, and factors that influence the effects of climate change have suffered changes, modifications dues as a consequence of the actions and/or omissions of the human being. They agreed that have occurred changes in the past as global warming and global cooling, but also, they accept that human beings have an important influence on the impact and the increasing negative impacts of climate change in the world.

Is not possible to deny that during the time of human beings, it has created and advanced in different areas as industries, business, and technology, as well in the use without moderation of different elements that not only have contributed to the advancement but also have contributed to increasing the level of contamination, toxic gases, that affects creating unexpected, unlimited, dangerous situations, and events around the world and it will continue affecting and producing deaths, destruction, and transformation of the environment for all living beings in the world.

With no recognition of the existence of climate change, these groups of scientists, members of society, and even researchers dismiss and reduce the importance of climate change, even when recognizing the existence of climate change their position is based on the that climate change always has existed and human beings do not have any responsibility, influence, or impact on the increase of the negative effect of climate change in the environment and all living being. Do not recognize climate change it has changed and the level of danger and risk has increased get justification by saying that these are events that always have occurred and will continue happening no matter what and human beings do not have anything to do with those changes based on situations and events occurred in the past.

In this group, it is possible to encounter contradictions between their justifications and allegations since when they recognize a part of the events and situations they deny other parts as if were two different situations that do not have any relation between them as it were tree and earth that have similarities and differences but only recognize the difference pleading that they are different and one does not affect the other when both depend of each other, the constant and multiple contradictions that they have demonstrated that their bases and principles are weeks due the denied to open to the situations and changes of the events, their positions in the majority of the cases are based on the existence of global warming and global cooling in the past, high and low temperatures, drought, flood, and don't evaluate the changes on periods, time, events, actions, from the past and present, only the previous existence of those events.

Do not know, do not understand, or do not have an interest in climate change, this third group is the one that generates the most preoccupation, and conflict between the two previous groups are trying to join the people that are in this group into their position convincing them that heir is right and the other one is wrong when in reality the people that do not have an interest or do not know, not understand what is climate change or effects of climate change because is not part of the priorities, life, or just because the way in how is being explained ad diffused the information is not easy to understand, manage by people that are not directly involved into the subject, even when it sound incredible to believes that the people who are part of this group, unfortunately, is the majority of the world population, due diverse circumstances or situations that is happening today.

But, what possible relation have those three groups' agreements and/or disagreement with climate change with the environment? is true that when is presented information, discussions, studies, research, and even debates only present the negative effects, and consequences that climate change is producing and will produce to human being life, risk, dangers, and not much about the danger and consequences that it produces to the environment, and all living beings in the world, studies of climate change demonstrate how the rise of temperature affect the ocean levels, increment of fire, drought, floods, temperatures but in the majority of the case in how that affects human life leaves very little information about the effects of climate change on the environment, as well the actions and/or inactions that have an influence on climate change those changes on climate change affect directly and not directly the environment showing that is a chain that joins human being – climate change – environment.

Climate change impact on the environment it is produced at a very rapid velocity in all directions without any distinction, producing changes in temperatures, level of ocean, amount and frequency of drought, floods, rain, storm, snow in the world but also it produce a change in the environment changing biological component in all forms of live from smallest microorganism to biggest animal, plants change patter of migrations, comportment of animals, development of plants, change in the weather, for example, snowing with more frequency in places where doesn't snow or don not snow with frequency, it also produce changes in the level of contamination, reduction of time that required the environment to complete all their process of evolution, as well it has produced changes in the behavior and migration in all animal species no matter where they are or their normal life movement and attitude, it has been possible to see in recent years how it has been an increase of a strange pattern, migrations out of time, loss of direction, increase of suddenly death of animals, many of those cases are being referred to different species of birds where the quality of air, and high temperatures on the sky it produces important effects that can be understanded.

Another case that can be mentioned corresponds to the aquatics animals that have and are suffering the changes in the density of the ocean, rivers, and lakes, where changes in the current pattern, storms, and temperature have created transformations in all aquatic life which it means a complete change in the aquatic life (ocean, rivers, lakes) environment which is not only a transformation it is also a challenge to all the professionals and not professionals that are involved directly and not directly in climate change and environment protection to identify and create the adequate strategies and mechanisms to carry on not only studies, and research, but also to prevent the increment of the negative events, situations, and changes, as be capable of follow the continuous challenges and understand which are and will be the present and future of all environment.

Climate Change has demonstrated the existence in the past, present, and future of many and diverse challenges that will never stop, the difficulty to carry on the studies and research at the same velocity that those changes occur is also a great challenge not only to professionals bound to the environment and climate change but also for the society who have a great percentage of people that are not directed linked to this two subjects or does not understand or have knowledge about them, having only suffered the consequences of the negative impacts, but:

- ✓ How it will be possible to go in a velocity capable to act in protecting of the environment and were of the negative impact of climate change?

No doubt that is a question that generate many discussions as many uncertain situations, considerations, and point of view not allowing in many cases react to a certain, possible, and positive answer or solution, statistics, numbers, percentages, videos, images are being presented every day, every hour, in every meeting, reunion, debate, discussion, wherever be possible to mention but what happen to the actions, is not only to recognize or not recognize the existence of climate change and the negative impacts, ins not only to know, accept or not accept how the effects of climate change influence and impact on the environment, and certainly is not only the presentation of statistics, number and percentage, there is many different positions, points of view but a reality that no on can denied is that all life in the world are suffering drastic changes unfortunately negative changes, and that is a call of attention to everyone to make adaptations to transforms that sadly and lamentable situation.

No matter if is being referred to as global warming, or global cooling, no matter is they are one group on the side of global warming and another on the side of global cooling all are part of the same group, and that group is "Climate Change and Environment", is not possible to separate climate change from the environment or separate environment from climate change, both are one, events that have occurred and by any circumstances can or can't happen again but they are part of the reality, part of the history that is the base of the climate change and the environment understand them, is only a step to understand, the changes and create the tools to protect and integrate with the environment.

Evaluation and Following, words that it has been used as excuses, and justifications for diverse situation that can results difficult, challenging and even not possible, but also is an important mechanisms that need to be carry on in ever steps of the follow of climate change and environment transformations, research, study, and capacity of creation and presentation of strategies that contribute to the transformation to the actual negative situation and start the process of reverse of them, accompanied with mechanism, that can survive through trough time and adapt to all the changes that occur in the present and can occur in the future, even when it has proved that not always evaluation and following has been capable to maintain in the time due circumstances on diverse country and/or global ambit it also important to not forget that this must be and obligation of all countries, national and international organizations, and NGOs to protect and maintain the correct, adequate, and necessary actions on climate change and the environment protection.

- ✓ How has been following the compliance of the sanctions?

The sanctions established in the legal norms, legislations, regulations, acts, and agreements have been imposed on those who do not comply and/or violet the legal norms, legislations, regulations, acts, and agreements? as well as every country has its own climate change and environment legal norms, legislations, regulations, acts, agreements also the International Organizations have international law, conventions, agreements that were signed by the different countries obligating them to comply whit those legislations, conventions, agreements, and legal norms making them also of obligatory accomplishment to business (national and/or international) industries (without distinction).

Climate Change and Environment are narrowly related, share many challenges, and events that need to be surpassed, but also have aspects that show the difference that exists between Climate Change and Environment producing that scientists, researchers, lawyers, jurists, professionals, and no professional linked directly with climate change and environment as well society, business, industries, and government have to work in this two subjects need to be studied and work on them separately due the difference and level of impacts that climate change produce and the environment suffer, the effects, also is the actions and omissions as well the existed and capable challenges that can appear, inside the particularities of climate change and environment.

Every strategy and mechanism that has been applied, proposed, and considered to be implemented in many aspects are statics not allowing flexibility and/or adaptation to the events and time, but they have the majority of the considerations made on human being protection and maintenance of human being exigencies, those strategies and planes have many points that are and can be contradictory between them even when their objective is focused in the reduction or elimination of the negative impacts of climate change and environment protection and survival.

- ✓ It is possible to consider strategies, and mechanisms to protect the environment separately from climate change and vice-versa?

This answer could result in complex and contradictory will a group say yes, a second group will say no, and even it appears a third group will say yes or no this last answer can confuse but makes sense due it can be created and proposed mechanisms, and strategies separately but no completely since in certain point it will produce an effect in both (climate change and environment).

It is possible to protect human beings without protecting the environment and reducing the negative effects of climate change? What is necessary to consider, is to reach society, to get all the sectors involved and comprised in the integration and protection of the environment and the reduction of the negative impacts of climate change, to carry knowledge and information to the society.

The world population to get to know and understand the meaning and importance of climate change and the environment, but only in an informal way through conferences, discussions, debates, webinars, seminars, and conversations but also formal education starting on the first levels to most high professional educational level in all areas, in all professions, inclusion must have to be the principal and primordial word in this process.

Integration and Protection of Environment

The integration with and protection of the environment are two important aspects in life that is not new or is a product of a research or technology is part of all life, and has existed since the origin of life and that have important challenges as is the technology, multiples questions accompany the relation between the human being and the environment, as well the integration of the human being with the environment, and the protection of the environment that must occur at every time, and moment without the existence of a calendar, program and/or chronogram to carry on this action and make it part of life.

- ✓ What is the meaning of integration?
- ✓ What is the meaning of protection?
- ✓ What is the relation between integration, protection, and environment?
- ✓ Why is important the protection of and integration with the environment?

Many are the aspects, events, and situations that surround the three aspects (integration, protection, and environment) separated and joined as one, but also is subjects of different positions are identified into three groups; the first group integrated with whom considered to understand and share the importance, and necessity of the environment, the second group conformed by who denies the existence and importance of the protection and integration of and with the environment, and the third group that doesn´t share any of the positions of the groups one and two and is integrated by whom don´t have any interest in the environment as in the protection and integration of and with the environment.

Those are only a few of the questions that are made in all sectors, in all levels, and in many cases in also all levels of education beginning in the first level of school when human beings start going through the obtention and increment of knowledge, as well in the educations, knowledge, and experience that who doesn´t have a formal education from school, education from school, education institutions, universities, and colleges the ate capably and have the skills, capacity, and ability to know and manage knowledge, situations, and events related to the environment, protection and integration of the environment that in many cases is not obtained through the formal education.

Integration and Protection are two powerful words that frequently is used and applied separately or are not considered as important in diverse ambits especially in the environment even more since the environment is seen as only a source of commodities and facilities for human beings, but:

- ✓ What is the real meaning of integration and protection?
- ✓ What do integration and protection for the environment and human beings?

They are more than only words to be used in speeches, discussions, debates, and even in studies, their meaning goes back to the recovering of connections, feelings, sensitivity, and life not only with the self-person but also with all life that surround the world as well as means protection of life in the present and future. Integration and protection are not an action that are temporary or momentary is an action, an activity that is constant and permanent not depend on the moment's attitude or the feelings at that time environment doesn't know about luxury, technology, or commodities, but does know about life, protection, security, health, food the most important aspect of life, so if the environment is capable of providing all those things:

- ✓ Why human beings cannot integrate with the environment and protect the environment from the damage that the same human beings are causing to the environment?

From the beginning of history and life always it has existed an important and almost indivisible relation between the environment and human beings just as it has existed protection from the environment to human beings and vice-versa, sadly as a consequence and result of different and multiple factors it has been influenced by the evolution and transformation of the world and society, this last one it got lost in time, transforming the protection that human beings given to environment into danger, destruction, and risk increment situation that unfortunately has persisted for a long time, and where the time has reached to reflection and impose the necessary, and indispensable to recover the integration and protection of the environment that has been lost.

Even with all the differences and particularities of the environment, is capable of working as one, as a team with perfect synchronization, and capacity of integration and incorporation which differs from human beings who have demonstrated difficulties in integrating and working as a team, joining as one leaving outside any differences, because skin color, race, sex, age, gender, religion, nationality, language, ethnicity capacity, level of knowledge, profession, increasing their reason to not accept and work as a team and unable to integrate and work together for the protection and of environment and life.

There is no doubt that is not an easy assessment to be capable of integrating and/or recovering the integration that was lost with the environment, making it more difficult and challenging, the amount of and in other cases is related to how beginning or starting from zero the integration with the environment, time and years pass, the separation and disconnection that human beings have with the environment, have increased. Another factor or element that can be mentioned is the loss of communication and is forgotten, human beings sadly have lost the sensitivity for all that surrounds them because the lifestyle, the indivisible independence for technology, and commodities that satisfy only a part of the daily activities, in occasions only to demonstrate that they can do it over or better than others or even do what others can't do or can do at a minor level or possibility, integration is more than the use and access to technology, commodities, and personal satisfactions, integration is recognition of the environment, sensibility to what surrounds the human being, recognition of the life that is in the environment, and the world, know this, accept and recognize this is only the first step of the many steps and challenges that need to surpass favor of the environment.

- ✓ Why the integration with the environment is important?

The answer to this question it not depends of one person or scientist, researcher, politic, government, or even from national and/or international organizations or institutions, or a group of environment activists in particular, on contrary it must be responded to by everyone, the answer to that question will not be easy to give to the question, it probably emerges with the other question:

- ✓ What sense does that have?

As it has more of a difference to what can be thinker on how to respond to those questions it will provide a new perspective, evaluation, and understanding of the environment and life as will be capable of understanding, and seeing what has been lost or hidden for a long time.

A very common and important word that represent actions is requested and demanded by all human being is ¨Respect¨, but also is requested and demanded by the environment and all life in the world, without any type of distinction or difference, and which needs and must be part of every activity and actions that is carried on every moment, the respect must exist not only between human beings it must also exists between human beings and the environment, and between human being and all life.

Respect is a word that has a special and important significance in the integration with the environment, respect to the environment, respect to all the elements that are part of the environment, and respect to life is not only said "I Respect" is also demonstrates it with actions, is not asking, requesting any type of economical action, or participation, is not required to enter in any action against the law, or life, by the contrary to any economical actions it required to comply, prove respect, fulfillment of the law and protection of life. Respect can be carried on with very little action, or activity, no omissions or evasiveness will create, generate, and increase the integrations with the environment is not necessary to carry on or complete any big action or activities that are outside the possibilities.

As consequence of the time, and distance that exists between the environment and human beings, it has caused that the capacity and possibility of the integration between the human beings and the environment are only capable of been possible partially and not completely increasing the challenges that the integration and relation between the environment and human beings is requested, is because of this that part of this integration process involves another action that comes with the integration end is the protection of the environment. It has been mentioned the existence of diverse legislations, international organizations, institutions, organizations, groups, and NGOs, are capable of protecting the environment themselves, so:

- ✓ Why human beings need to integrate and protect the environment?

Is those legislations that have demonstrated the capacity to protect the environment by themselves, but even when they have a certain level of advantages contrary to what they want or they are, they also have demonstrated that do not have the capacity and qualifications to protect the environment by themselves and require the incorporation and participation of all human beings to protect the environment, being now is the time when all human being needs to join and protect the environment and for this is no excuse or say “I don’t know how possible or accepted”.

When it comes to the moment to evaluate and implement actions, and strategies to prevent events and situations that are needed for the protection of the environment is important and indispensable to recognize that every action no matter the size of every legislation, in every campaign, obtention of knowledge, and diffusion of information that is carried on, for that exist many strategies, mechanisms, and methods that can be applied to protect and integrate with the environment and obtain the expected, required, and needed results.

Everyone (scientists, lawyers, legislators, politics, government, educators, business, society, kids, youth, adults, professionals, no professionals) has an important role in the integration of environment protection, where inaction is no part of it, each one inside the one capacity and knowledge it provides the tools that combined will create important action impacting the environment, not only locally, but also globally, always remembering that what affect or prejudice the environment in one place it will affect negatively the environment in all the world not only in that place, making necessary and indispensable for the protection of the environment in one place it will be reflected in the world, the environment and life. When reading and listening to declarations, discussions, debates, and information about the environment is very common to listen:

> "We need to protect the environment today
> for the present and future generations"

Unfortunately, the integration and protection of the environment is a subject that has been taken and transformed into a political and economic subject of exploitation without being taken seriously and given the importance that really needs, it has been converted into a political speech with empty words, and empty meaning when the time of action has reached and passed, the question emerges:

- ✓ What happened with that speech in which it referred to environmental integration and protection?
- ✓ What do you do to protect and integrate with the environment?

It results how the growing consideration, belief, and thinking of Human Beings regarding obligations and responsibilities where those only exist for human beings and not for human beings to the environment and all life in the world, and to see how the responsibility and obligation of integration and protection of the environment have become a chain reaction to pass it from person to person, sector to sector of passing the responsibility and obligation of environmental protection.

The existence, and survival of the environment is not a subject that is not submitted to discuss its importance, relevance, and necessity for the survival of all life including human beings, is not a subject of discussion that the environment is united with all life not only animals, plants, and microorganisms, but also with human beings is a chain where the environment, humans, animals, plants, and microorganisms all life depend on each other they are not separated or independent from each other, the survival integration and protection of the environment is the survival of all life, the question.

- ✓ How it will be possible to integrate and protect the environment?

Questions that it has and is being asked to scientists, lawyers, jurists, researchers, politicians, environment groups national and international organizations NGOs, as also society, in general, will give a response that will from the simplest to the more technical, scientific, and legal answer which many people don't know and/or do not understand, as also is possible to obtain answer with a simple language capable to reach to all, and some actions that in occasions are not the correct type of actions, in occasions seen how to justify the violent protest and/or actions to demonstrate the importance of the environment protection but not forgetting that acts of violence and vandalism only carry the environment protection in a different direction.

- ✓ Is only needed to dedicate a small time to reflect on what is the environment. How important is the environment?

The relation and dependence of human beings on to environment also help to understand why is so important the protection of the environment and to start taking conscience and action to contribute to environment integration and protection, with actions that can go from the smallest to the biggest and complex action, without not incurring into negative or bad actions, and activities that instead of protecting the environment it will create more damages to environment and life.

- ✓ How it will be possible to carry on actions to protect the environment without falling into negative actions/activities?

It depends on society, scientists, lawyers, and jurist researchers to evaluate, consider, and implement the appropriate actions/activities to protect and integrate with the environment without producing a negative reaction, situation, and/or event that wasn't considered when was created, drafted the strategies, actions that have, are, or want to be implemented.

The integration and protection of the environment not represent only a subject to be studied in schools and/or in a professional career, it is seen on TV, in documentaries, or news, is a work of obtention of knowledge, reading information about what is the environment, knowing or saying that know the importance of the integration and protection of the environment is, and how is proposing or carrying on diverse actions, it is also to put in practice all the knowledge, information, but must important the feeling and sensitivity in the integration whit and protection of the environment, and which it also depends on how it will be capable to be part of it.

One of the most important and indisputable failures and challenges that exist between human beings, the environment, and life is how human beings are always asking for more actions, and developments to provide commodities and facilities that help them to comply with their work necessities, and continue to carry on their lifestyle, but as while human beings are constantly asking for those actions and developments it also needs to be capable of measuring the consequences of those requirements, and exigencies, and how it can obtain their exigencies without affecting the environment, and life, the human being needed to be capable of measuring the level of exigencies, results, and consequences, need to be capable to live and shares with the environment in a healthy, balanced and equitable way, where the environment does not be affected negatively, and can continue growing, living through time, and giving life to all living being in the world.

The protection and integration with the environment today and always are going to be an obligation that all have to comply is not a selective or optional activity or action that human beings can choose to carry on, and neither is an occasional, permanent, constant, and daily obligation that the no complement it will and can produce negative impact and consequences to the environment, human being, and all life, being possible to implement sanctions to the actions and omissions.

A very important lesson that the environment has given to human beings is tightly related to the not for even that human beings suffer as a consequence of the pandemic caused by COVID-19 has shown how the actions and omissions of human beings affect negatively the environment, and how small time of change in the working of industries, businesses, and human being activities was capable of producing changes on the Environment even when occurs for a little period of time in all the levels, animals, plants, elements (air, water, earth, fire, temperatures) around the world, if that occurs with a little time, what can happen with an integrated and united collaboration of all countries, human beings, business, industries, government (All sectors) in the world for the Environment integration and protection. Some examples that occur during the pandemic of COVID-19 are cases of when animals entering the cities, ocean animals that return to places from where they haven´t been seen in a long time, changes in the color of the rivers water, changes in the air, and the level of contaminations, many of those events was recorded on videos that were shared and seen around the world showing that human beings are doing something wrong, and needs to take actions to transform those negative actions and activities.

The common interest in survival is one of the pilar that move and motivate scientists, lawyers, jurists, and researchers to act in the reduction and/or elimination of the negative impacts of climate change and the integration and protection of the environment, but it results not be sufficient the interest of survival which can have many different obstacles, difficulties, and contradictions, it is also necessary to count on other aspects that keep the interest of survival, depending on who is asking it will give different answers mostly directly in the professional ambit, or the curiosity area but leaving outside the most important of all which is no other than the essence of life the integration and protection of the environment it carries no only to protect living being but also carry to the essence of life in all of the highest levels.

Globalization and the Integration and Protection of the Environment

According to the necessity, or area is possible to encounter different types of globalization definitions, some of them are presented by the dictionaries in a simple way to be understood, and many other definitions that exist today have been developed around sectors such as economy, business, and industries, but the meaning of globalization goes much further from the economic sector and also is related to other areas such as education, communication, professional, research, which it give another sense of the initial ideal with which it born the globalization it opens a new definition transforming the initial objective, creating a new vision, objective, definition of globalization being capable to defined as the interconnection that reduces berries, conflicts, distance and increase opportunities of advancements and development for all the countries in all the sectors.

The born of globalization occurs not as a consequence of the changes in the world and society but as a result of the necessity of a change where it is possible to reduce and eliminate distance, barriers, and limitations being capable of producing opportunities and advancements for all the countries in all sectors actors according to their requirements, and conditions, also it has as one of their objectives the union of efforts to protect the environment and all life in the world, unfortunately as the globalization are capable of producing positive results and possibilities it also it has been used to create and increase damage, danger and affect in a very negative way the environment and all life in the world.

The globalization is not static, is always changing and suffering transformations as a result of their integration and dependency on technology, which makes globalization dynamism is every day more complex and challenging and capable of suffering disruptions that can result in the rise of difficulties, situations, and events that needs to surpass, affecting and making unsuccessful to comply with success, efficiency and efficacy the globalization objectives, also been possible to observe how globalization have some very weak strategies and mechanisms that affect negatively the stability, present and future of globalization.

With the passing of time and adaptation, globalization has become an important, and indivisible part of life, reducing and eliminating distance, as well as providing the opportunity to increase possibilities in diverse areas, growing communications, interactions, exchange of knowledge, experiences, and expertise regarding the integration and protection of the environment, also it has influenced the production of diverse and multiple impacts on the environment and incrementing the challenges and difficulties for the protection of the environment.

- ✓ What does it mean for globalization to the integration and protection of the environment?
- ✓ How globalization is capable of promoting and increasing the integration and protection of the environment?
- ✓ How does globalization affect negatively the integration and protection of the environment?

A difference with other questions that involve globalization is that those questions have a particular direction and effect, as a consequence of the fundaments, direction, and objective as well as looking to how globalization will be capable of increasing the efforts and getting more involved in the integration with, and the protection of the environment, and from which it is also to see the merging of diverse positions, points of view, perspectives, and considerations, some that show agreements and others where it is contradictions and disagreements, but in every case, they will in the importance and transformation that globalization has produced in the world, no doubt that globalization it is very important to all the countries through cooperation, economic growth, advancements in all the different ambits, it also has produced important damage to the environment, increasing the danger and affected all living being.

The studies, research, evaluations, and recommendations that have been carried on regarding globalization have primarily focused on what is capable of offering to human beings, the characteristics and capacities of globalization to obtain a major level of benefit forgetting and leaving aside the negative side the negative impact that the globalization is capable to and produce in the present and future, in a short, medium, and long period of time which can also be classified and/or divided as direct and/or not direct.

- ✓ Damage
- ✓ Destruction
- ✓ Risk increment
- ✓ Death

- ✓ Trafficking
- ✓ Climate Change Impact
- ✓ Extinction

Destruction of the environment, it results contradictory to see how globalization is capable of reducing and eliminating barriers and limitations is also capable of causing and increasing the destruction of the environment, a situation that in a very high percentage is not recognized or accepted by the diverse sectors that are part of the globalization, because is not considered as important or relevant, because is against the economics benefits or human beings necessities and priority, situations, and allegations that every day are more common and frequent without seeing any type of actions or impositions of sanctions to stop the environment destruction. There are multiple examples of environment destruction in forests, oceans, rivers, lakes, mountains, and deserts, is not possible to mention one area or place where the environment is not subject to destruction without any observation or interest in changing that situation.

Trafficking, is not possible to mention one single action or activity that is not related to trafficking, and involves the environment, animals, and all types of life that exist in the world, and sadly is necessary to say that globalization has contributed to increasing this terrifying activity, been in many cases not capable to be detected and/or stopped, due lack of interest, not giving the importance and relevance that deserve or because doesn´t have the mechanisms, capacity, and support necessary and indispensable to combat this not legal actions, and activities that put in danger and affect negatively the environment and life.

Death of multiple and different species of animals, and plants, is a very negative impact that globalization produces it can be observed in the high numbers and velocity with which increase the death of the different species of animals, plants, and all environment life without any remorse and/or intention of stopping this situation, and demonstrating that the globalization only has two objectives, ideas and direction as are the economics benefits and human being lifestyle, creating as consequence a disbalance on the life cycle, and producing new challenges for the survival together with more difficulties and obstacles to the challenges that already exists needs to surpass.

Contribution to the change of animals migration, exploitation and damage of animals, natural environment, the animals migration is another negative side of the globalization where the changes of animals migration it has been produced as consequence of the exploitation of animals, as well as the exploitation of the environment using as excuse the accomplishment of the globalization objectives and compromises that was acquired through the different agreements subscribed and signet for the success of globalization, and where it not has been measured the consequence and impact that produce the animals migrations pattern , the exploitation of animals, plants, and all environment, how those actions affects in short, medium and long period of time, being possible to observe, determine, and stablish that those changes and exploitations activities affects all life survival, as the evolution affecting also the globalization in a negative way, making it more difficult and challenging to survive and be capable of maintain in the present and future.

The primary and principal objective of globalization is economic benefit regarding which actions are taken and/or carry on to obtain the results expected and wanted, even when it represents to affect the environment and all life in the world, but also it have demonstrated that despite all the agreements, contracts, and/or conventions tan can be mentioned in relation to globalization there are very and/or haven't do any action to change that negative impact, even when globalization is not referred to a specific person or human beings, group nationals or international organization, industry, business, or government it doesn't means that it don't have obligations, responsibilities and is capable to be imposed sanctions, by the contrary as is referred to globalization everyone, country, government, business, industries, national and international organizations, person or human being share the same responsibility, obligation, and capacity to impose a sanction to protect the environment, making necessary to the globalization and all the sectors that direct and not directly are involved in the different areas of globalization to promote, create, develop, implement supervise, and guarantee the creation, adaptation of the necessaries measures to transform and stop all those actions and activities that affect and impact negatively in the environment and all life in the world, but also to assure that those measures be capable to perdure in the time and don't become unsuccessful.

Extinction can be mentioned as one of the most delicate, notable, and less care of all the negative impacts that produce globalization to the environment and all life in the world and, also is the one that at every hour, every minute increases the extinction of an important number of animal species and all different type of environment life many of them know, not knowing, identified and not identified or classified by the knowledge only by very little documentation or research but with the increasing of the levels of extinction it will be not possible to get to know them as well it will not be possible to know and/or identified the advantages and possibilities that they could be possible, as the risk that life can suffer as a consequence of the extinction of animal species and environment.

As well as protection is part of globalization it also integration with the environment is also an important part of globalization since with the base and principle of integration and protection of the environment, globalization will be capable of continuing to advance, grow, and develop new mechanisms for the present and future protecting life, through the integration and protection of the environment, and it will give origin to new possibilities, and capacities where the combination and union of all to protect, maintain and allow to continue advancing the globalization becomes one of the priorities for human beings, countries, and environment.

Is not possible to say that globalization refers to only one specific sector, on contrary it is important to maintain, protect, and continue advancing in the strengthening of globalization in the present and future is also important and urgent that it be taken measures to globalization starts, continues, and deepen the integration and protection of the environment as well collaborate in the reduction, and eliminations of those elements that produce and increase contamination and deaths.

Collaboration, participation, and integration are three of the multiple actions that globalization needs to take, promote, and carry on to integrate with and protect the environment from all the negative impacts, damage, and danger that are suffering, and from situations and/or events that can occur in the future, create and implement strategies, mechanisms that are based in the collaboration, participation, and integration through the principles, objectives, and direction of the globalization it will increase the possibilities of obtention success in the integration and protection of the environment.

As with all developments, globalization doesn't escape having challenges and difficulties due to the existence of difficult, hard situations in many countries which generate problems to continue advancing, an example of that can be observed due to conflicts, wars, and as a consequence of the effects suffered as a result of the pandemic occurred by COVID-19 creating problems to maintain globalization but even whit those situations globalization it doesn't stop as either the negative impact on the environment that is why is so important the incorporation and use of the globalization in the protection of the environment, which it will transform the negative impact, negative situation in both into positive results.

Challenges of the Integration and Protection of the Environment

Even when it exists many indisputable, and important reasons for which the is necessary, and indispensable the integration of human beings with the environment, as well as the protection of the environment, is not possible to deny that there also exists and will exist a diversity of challenges to surpass, which are and will not be easy due many and different circumstances that are present every day and that in occasions it will show a no imaginable force to divert and make forget the environment trying to prioritize other aspects and trying to make see that the environment is not and/or less important than the others aspects or situations. Those challenges are present in all sectors not only in personal life and/or society is also is present in the professional ambit, as business, industries, economy, political, legal, government, activists, national and/or international organizations, and NGOs.

Personal Life is no discussion that all people have a personal life with necessities, ambitions, obligations, and responsibilities which on many occasions cover all the time leaving very little time to even take the time to rest and recover energy, situations that produce a wall or block on what is surrounding the person not allowing to see or appreciate the sound of the birds in the morning, a time of relax in a park or even to see the stars through the windows making it one of the most complex and difficult challenge that human beings have to be capable of integrating with the environment, in occasions feelings also have a big influence in these situations contributing to increased separation, isolation, and loss of communication, connection, and integration with the environment, time in the personal life it is also something that is difficult accomplish and have a distribution of time that allow to comply with all the activities without any problem, or an unexpected event or situation, allow to incorporate a new activity as is the integration with the environment and protection of the environment.

- ✓ How it will be possible to integrate and protect the environment with personal life activities today when there are complications?

Is not asking too much to incorporate in the personal life the integration and protection of the environment? those are two of the most common, critical, and maybe whit more conflicts that are present when is direct this topic to a person, and that will give origin to an unlimited question, reasons, excuses, and justifications some with reason and others without any reason and/or justification possible.

Today is possible to see how personal life and activities are surrounded by technology (hobbies, games, sports, music, distraction, family time, work/job, studies) and how much time is dedicated to complying the personal life activities without technology, is no doubt that technology offers important help in some aspects but, is also true that have contributed to transforming life and increasing the separation between people and between human beings and the environment, with life, no doubt that is challenging that every human being needs to reflect and learn how to create a balance between personal life – technology – environment, and understand that environment is part of the life of every human being (person) and without life and that connection, integration, and protection of the environment it not going to be life, and even is not going to be any technology that can be enjoyed and/or exist.

Society is a sector with great influence on a human being (image, friends, activities, clothes, technology, economic capacity, luxury) and many other aspects that can be included, society has become one of the biggest rulers of life even if it recognized or not, and that lifestyle established by the society it has produced that is the environment is who suffer the consequences, the effects of that competency, rivalry that the society has created in all the world, is not possible to say that is a country safe of the society rule, is not possible to say that society has not promoted the destruction, and damage of the environment, and even increased the levels of risk and dangers, but contrary to what it is thought not all society have the same level of fault or can be blamed, there are different level of responsibilities.

Society is also divided into different groups according to economic level, social position, lifestyle, knowledge and/or education level race, or religion, and many other aspects that have influenced the evolution, development, and capacity of survival of human beings, but also it has influenced on how it will respond differently to the environment, and which respond to the environment with questions such as:

- ✓ Which should I care about the environment?
- ✓ If I say something or do something that involves the environment, I am going to be famous?
- ✓ Is going to help me gain popularity?
- ✓ I am going to have any economic earnings?

Between the different aspects that are related to the society and the environment, as well as the questions that were presented before it is possible to observe how those are some of the most common and popular questions that are found in society leaving little sectors of society, as well as the existence of other questions such as:

- ✓ How I can help to protect the environment?
- ✓ What is the environment?
- ✓ How I can integrate with the environment?

- ✓ What does integration and protection of the environment mean?

But even when is a small group it means that there is hope, and it means that they need to reunite and create a strong force to reach, include, and incorporate every hour, every day more and more people, transforming the actual meaning of society, and transforming this rule into a new rule where incorporate the environment, protect life and reduce the damages, risks, and deaths of all living being in the world.

Business, involves different sectors of the country and interests, due to their major compromise with a certain level of advancement depending on the business size, capacity, and area, but in every case, the major direction is related to obtaining a major economic position, winnings on which on no moment take into consideration how their activity can affect directly and/or not directly the environment. Businesses today are looking to not continue being local or working in a specific location they are looking to expand themselves in the biggest possibilities whether is the national level or the international ambit, or even in both only making reference tan taking into consideration the legislations and legal norm that are considered as directly referred to the type of business, which not always include obligations and responsibilities concerning the environment.

Is very common to see in actuality how the majority of the different businesses include any types of actions, or measures, to the integration and protection of the environment, forgetting and leaving in one side the influence that the business has no matter the location, the role of business it has been considered thoroughly as an exchange of product, merchandise and/or service for an amount of money but business is more than that, it represents the possibilities of advancements, opportunities, changes that can be positive and/or negative for human being as well as for the environment and all living being.

- ✓ How a small business as a store can have an impact on the environment?
- ✓ How a business (small, medium, or big size) can contribute to the protection of the environment?
- ✓ How a business (small, medium, or big size) can integrate with the environment?

- ✓ Are the environment legislations establishing obligations, responsibilities, and sanctions to businesses (small, medium, or big size)?

Some of the questions that many businesses that exist in the world as the different parts (direct and/or direct) involved with the business have fallen in the error of not being made or considered, and the answers will produce surprise, doubts, and no doubt more questions due to the lack of knowledge of this side of business.

Businesses are capable of producing a negative impact on the environment, increasing the damage, risk, and unexpected situations probably what they consider is not important and/or relevant but continuously committing the same actions and carrying on the same attitude increases the negative impact, that is why is important a change on business integrating them into the environment and protecting the environment with different types of actions, strategies, and mechanisms.

Industries, don't have the same obligations, responsibilities, and sanctions as businesses. Yes, industries and businesses share some of the same obligations, responsibilities, and sanctions making the difference present in the size, what makes industries have major obligations and responsibilities, and capable of suffering different types of sanctions, but also is important not to forget the type of material the industries use for their production, generating a major negative, and damage to the environment and the life of all living being in the world, as well as the industries should comply with the national legislations, legal norms, regulations also are obligate to comply with the international legislations, legal norms, agreements conventions, that was signed concerning industries and the environment protection.

- ✓ What makes different industries different from business?

If it is considered from a general perspective it is necessary to say that industries and business are two sectors completely different due to size, localization, type of work, production, number of employees, capacity of places where they reach, materials, and technology that are used, but if is reviewed and analyzed from the point of the integration and protection of the environment the answer it will be that they are no different they are equal industries and business have the same obligations and responsibilities to protect the environment.

Due to the characteristics and particularities of the industries they have a major challenge to change their work, actions, activities, materials, and manner or production in a way that allows them to continue having the same capacity, and protect the environment which is the major excuse used by the industries to not compromise and change, as well as costs of doing those changes, when in reality is not so difficult and impossible to do those changes and the cost on the contrary of producing damages to the industries it will increase their possibilities, development, and advancement in the present and future, as well it will produce an important impact in the reduce of contamination, the expulsion of contaminant that affect the environment and life and change it into increasing of protection of environment and life of all living being in the world.

Economy, the sector is divided into two groups the first group is related to the society and individual economy of business, industries, and society in an individual position, and the second group is directed to the country's economy, in the case of the first group is necessary to mention the fluctuant, changing, unstable factors that are present in all the countries in national and international level, affected by the multiple events that occur every day in the world and where the economy is based on national and international markets can produce instantly changes, in the case of the society, person their economy can be complex as a consequence of the different economic capacity what has divided the society on poor class, middle class, and high class what give origin to increase the separation, losses the communication and integration with the environment.

As well as the protection of the environment those economic difficulties and differences in the society have also create a barrier that covers almost all the time and aspects of life, but also affect the possibilities of improvement, and advancements, in the case of the second group that I referred to the country economy is more complex than the first group due the different and numbers of compromises, obligations and manner in how is managed the economy to comply with success and efficiency their national and international obligations and responsibilities, which it doesn't exempt to the country to comply with the national and international legislations, legal norms, agreements, and conventions to protect the environment the major ones responsible for guaranteeing the protection of the environment not only by the country but also by the country's economic sector and society, conflicts (national and/or international) war, changes in the economy, migrations climate change risks, are only a few aspects that make a country economy unstable no matter if is referred to a developed or no developed country.

At the stage of the evaluation, and follow the economy as one of the challenges that the integration and protection of the environment requires considering internal and external factors, situations, and events, but also obligated to consider to evaluate the dispositions of the two groups into compromise and compliance with the environment protection since it can be required to make changes and adaptations that society, people, business, industries, government, countries are not willing to do alleging many reasons that it doesn't have bases to sustain.

Political, is an aspect that always had, and it will continue to produce discussions, contradictions, confrontations, and even be difficult to reach a point of accordance or is the case that is no reach to accordance due to the considerations of what they considered as a priority to manage, all the political groups have what they consider their priorities or situations that need to the first subjects to manage where in very few cases are found the environment protection, that situation is produced by the called traditional or known political groups it has given origin in many countries to what is known as green political groups or political party who their principal proposal or direction is based on the environment protection, political party or group that it doesn't escape of having problems, and don't comply in all the cases with the objective that make the create the green political group or political party, as also they haven't be capable of gain popularity and acceptation in the society making them in some countries to disappear as they impossibility or lack of capacity to continue carrying their voices in national and international level and being known.

The political sector reunites different points of view, considerations, works, and trajectories, and is always in constant transformation as the world and society continue changing affecting all the countries, including those countries that today continue having the monarchy or royal as the head of the country, where they are being affected and requiring changes as is it possible to see how it has been questions as if is today necessary to continue having the royal or monarchy as a head of the country or they need to change ad adapt to the rest of the countries political system? other questioning and considerations in this subject has born as the change of time, changes of society, but also are who want to maintain the royalty or monarchy as a head of the country which create a discussion, and debates concerning the future of the country political situation.

Legal, is probably the sector with fewer advancements and challenges regarding the integration and protection of the environment, exist multiple aspects that make to legal sector fail as not enough legal professionals (lawyers, jurists, researchers) in the environment area, lack of legislations, the priority of environmental law, time that is taken to redact, discuss, approve, an entry into effect the environment legislation, legal norm, regulation, by the time when those legislations enter in effect the is occurring new events, situations that make necessary to reform the legislation, legal norm, and/or regulations, another aspect that is not favorable in the legal ambit is that environment is not considered as a priority as well many countries do not have the team necessary to carry on the research, evaluation and follow of the environment and be capable to work with the legal team.

The legal sector doesn't escape contradictions, discussions, and even misappreciation, or no understanding of the importance of environment law, multiple countries face a lack of motivation, and rueful development, and work in this area has been increasingly negative making it more difficult to transform this situation into more incorporation in the environment law, as is also necessary to increase the velocity and reduce the time in the redact, discuss, approve, and enter in effect the environment legislations, legal norm, regulations, agreements, and conventions.

The legal sector has many important failures and challenges to surpass and that must start in the universities, schools of law, and even in the law bar where they have failed to motivate and integrate future law professionals into environment law.

- ✓ How those failures can be changed, transformed, and integrated in this area of Law?

Another aspect is the lack of the existence of environment courts (national and international) which increases the opportunity, and possibilities to not recognize, disclaim, and not comply with the environment legislations under the security of no existence or little existence of environment court of justice, as the difficulty to probe the damage caused and time that takes to carry an environment case to a national and/or international court.

Activists, together with the political sector the activist conforms one of the most controversial and difficult sector for the integration and protection of the environment, in the world it has been possible to see and know the existence of different activists that proclaim to be against the environment destruction, and by the contrary theme try to protect the environment, some of this activists groups have many years of existence and other activist groups have more recent data, in both cases the carry on different actions, activities to call the attention but unfortunately many of those activities goes much more that incentivize the integration and protection of the environment by the contrary some of them fall in not adequate or correct actions causing damages and increasing a negative acceptation or reception in those activists as individually and group, another aspects that produce a negative acceptation and take back the possible positive advancements is how many activities carry on activities or actions that goes contrary to what they say or proclaim creating a controversy on what is saying and what are doing, situations that activist groups can have important and clear objectives, principles, directions but also they faces an important weakness as major number of member they have more difficult is to control and or reduce those negative actions that create more negative impact and effects.

Other aspects that involve the environment activist refer people of the society, individuals who are not members of any activist group, and also carry on activities that do not have any organization and/or direction that protect the environment without being capable of obtaining the results expected in totally or partially, what makes them reduce their actions and activities until the point that are very little the actions or information about them on the diverse information sources, increasing the disappointment, confrontations between them, and failure.

National and International Organizations, the actions of the national and international organizations look to cover diverse areas in which compromise all the countries to get involved in the protection of the environment through legislations, conventions, agreements, conferences, education, and other types of actions and collaborations between countries and between national, and international organizations and the countries, but those actions it can get compromised and reduce the velocity increasing the time that it will take to complete them and for obtain the expected results, and as well as possible that those projects or proposal not be approved or get canceled due controversies, conflicts, or disagreement in a certain point due aspects or subjects that it wasn't considered or taking into consideration, but also due disagreement between the parts that are involved directly and not directly in those project, proposal or action, situation that only produce more damage and backward in the environment protection.

National and International Organizations have an important role and a powerful voice in the world in some subjects but in others, as is the environment faces many difficulties, and challenges that can result bigger than the capacity that those national and international organizations have, no matter the size, powerful or name of those organizations that have problems in areas as lack of professionals, integration with society, incorporations of professionals, management of situations in the countries, making them suffer rejections, and reductions of possibilities, capacities, qualifications, acceptance, also reducing the possibilities, and capacity of response and act on time, increasing the breaches, challenges, difficulties, and problems to solve instead of advancements, doesn't mean that they have produced important actions through time and have redacted, signed and on comes into effect important legislations, conventions, agreements, achieving that the majority of the countries sign them on the different areas. Still, it also has important failures following the compliance of those legislations, conventions, and agreements, reducing the damage to the environment, preventing the production and causes of more damage to the environment, and implementing the corresponding sanctions.

Surpassing the Challenges of the Integration and Protection of the Environment

What mean to surpass the challenges of the integration and protection of the environment? Is it only to create strategies to solve problems and/or surpass the challenges? The answer to those questions and many more questions like those depends on each and everyone but is important to always remember that the human being always is going to be linked to the environment, it depends on how is accepted, integrated, and capable of reconnecting and communicate with the environment is when the difference it will begin in each one and individually and in groups as a team it will create the changes regarding the integration and protection of the environment, those should not only be questions, it must be a reflection and a change on the actions, attitudes, and omissions of the human beings.

Is not possible to denied that the integration and protection of the environment is a subject with a great complexity, amplitude surrounded with diverse, and multiple series of situations, events, challenges on different ambits, and sectors, also face challenges with all the actors that have interest, do not have interests, are directly involved, are not directly involved with the integration and protection of the environment, situations, contradictions, conflicts, wars, discussions, debates and many other things that can be mentioned, projects, proposals, actions, activities that has been carry on in the past, and the present, that have started and haven obtained the expected results, that it wasn't capable to be completed, that have been started and still are working on them, that still need time to be completed, that is going to start, or have been stopped, actions, and activities by the society, by the activist, and the different sectors (national and international) all and everyone them without any possible exception have demonstrated to have failure, challenges to surpass, and have weakness, but that doesn't means that those challenges cannot be surpassed and obtain success, but it is an important and no unrecognizable call of attention of it is necessary to detect, evaluate where is the failure and strategies, mechanisms, action's needs, and can be taken to correct that weakness, failure.

As is true that many and multiple challenges the integration and protection also exist numerous and important strategies, mechanisms, and tools in all the different sectors that can be used, and implemented to surpass those challenges, there is no possibility to say I don't have the tools and/or mechanisms, or even to say I can't, I don't know how, every person have an incredible capacity to work and to make things possible as well as to connect, and integrate with the environment and protect the environment from any type of damage and/or danger, is also necessary to remember, recognize and recover that connection, that integration with environment and life that it got lost or more to say it was in a profound stage of sleepiness.

Education, communication, and integration are three important words in the process of surpassing the challenges in the integration and protection of the environment, and there emerges the question.

- ✓ How education, communication, and integration will be capable of surpassing the integration and protection of the environment with all differences such as distance, language, country challenges, and conflicts?

There is no doubt that situations that don't make capable of reaching all the countries in the world due to the existence of conflicts and/or were but also true that not all countries face the same situations, in the case of the countries that are not facing conflicts and/or war it is possible to reach to them with and without the use of technology, creating strategies that include the society, and in the case of those countries that unfortunately are facing conflicts and/or war it is important to remember that the conflicts and/or war cannot last all life and for when finishing it star the moment of recovering the country, life, and environment and for that, they will need all the possible help including all the educations, information, communication that exist to the able and capable of recuperate their country environment and life.

In actuality exists many strategies, and mechanisms, that can be applied to surpass the integration and protection of the environment, on some occasions, it will be necessary to stop thinking locally and/or nationally and review, study, exchange information, knowledge, experience with other countries, other sectors not only the one who is directly involved or are inside the activist group, national and international organizations, government, economic, politic, scientist, and or legal sector is also necessary to involve all the society integrate the society into the environment and integrate the society into the actions, and activities for the protection of the environment.

Research and follow, are two strategies that can result in challenges but are capable of providing important information capable to reducing the difference in time between the environment and the different sectors, allowing also to obtain knowledge and capacity to understand the changes that are happening in the present and can happen in the future, what the research and follow it will be also possible to determine which are from the less to the most dangerous factors that affect the environment and how they change, and evolution.

The research and following it also provide the mechanisms, information, and tools to understand, evaluate, and control the level of impact, and damage caused to the environment as a consequence of the actions and omissions caused by human beings, and the different sectors, which is one of the most difficult, complex, and controversial challenges that need to be surpassed by everyone, everywhere, to protect the environment, using different and various tools that involve the use and not use of technology it can help to complete the actions, as well as to create new mechanisms and incentivize the collaboration and participation of all sectors in national and international level.

Actions, when thinking about how to surpass the integration and protection of the environment start whit thoughts, ideas, plans, sketches, but is very frequent that it only reach until there, not being capable to advance to the next step of the process and reach to the action, to the practice, and implementation, situation that many different factors can cause, and there is where is the difference between the actions and the omissions in the integration and protection of the environment, is very common to believe or consider that only the actions that reach to a high level as politics sectors, government, national and international organizations is what it will provide the changes necessaries, but by the contrary all actions that are carry on from the smallest to the biggest it create the steps necessaries to surpass the challenges of the integration and protection of the environment is no matter if is locally (in the area where live, or work) or is in the community, in the job/work, those actions are going to produce a chain reaction that will spread and grow, the important is to complete the actions and not fall into the omissions and inactions.

Strategies, every project, action, work/job that going to be done to protect the environment requires a strategy that can guarantee the completion of the objectives and implement those strategies with efficacy, efficiency, and adaptability to ensure their durability in time and not be lost with the changes and/or transformations of the world and be capable of obtain the expected results, and success, it is indispensable that the strategies don't be statistics by contrary be capable of change and suffer reforms, adaptations but never losing the essence, base, and principles with which was created and/or implemented those strategies on the first time.

Determination, one of the most difficult aspects, feelings, and attitudes to maintain when is necessary to surpass a challenge as big as is the integration and protection of an environment that is full of new changes, events, situations, constant movements, and transformations that can create more challenges but, those situations is what must give the strength to maintain and increase the determination of the integration and protection of the environment, what it is important is not give up always think in how beautiful, and gorgeous is the environment and how important is for life.

Conclusion

The integration and protection of the environment is a topic of great importance for the survival of all living beings in the world and it has been reduced to only a specific group forgetting that is a matter of interest for all human beings, and for every sector of development it also important to remember that is not a distinction between countries developed or not developed, many are the challenges, difficulties, problems that surround the integration and protection of the environment but it also is present opportunities, possibilities, and actions that are and can been carried on.

Diverse sectors in the ambit related to the economy, politics, legal, government, social, individual, educational, and technological have been mentioned with possibilities and benefits as well as the damage and danger that they mean and produce to the environment, not forgetting that well as they and their advancement are necessary to human beings is important and indispensable that they comply with the obligations, and responsibilities to protect the environment and in the case of failure been capable of suffer the sanctions that have been established in the national and international legislations, always remembering that no one escape of their obligation with the environment and life.

The actions and omissions that human beings do or don't make affect all life living beings in the present and the future it depends on all as a team to work to protect life and be capable of survival leaving one side those positions that increase difference, restrictions, and danger, today human beings live in a world that has reduced or eliminated barriers in many sectors, but also it has created an increased barriers, in many other areas increasing may sad situations and conflicts forgetting the reals essence of integration, cooperation, and life.

Challenges, strategies, mechanisms, and possibilities have been mentioned, but these are only a few of them, there exist many others and with every day that passes they increase and change, and suffer modifications, transformations producing more and different situations and events in the worlds, each one of them represents in the present and future a very important call of attention about what is wrong, what human beings are making wrong, where human beings are failing and the importance of change that negative conduct, that wrong attitude into a conduct an attitude that allows life to growth and evolution.

Numerous questions were presented one with answers simpler than others, some questions can be considered as statics or with non-validity in the present or for the future, while others are capable of originating more diverse questions, doubts, and even reflection on how the changes have an impact on the attitude and conduct of human beings not only between human beings but also with the environments, and all life creating a breach that has been capable of causing danger and damage to all living beings around the world without any type of hesitation.

Is important to always remember that every day, every hour, and every minute is a new opportunity that human beings have to reconnect and integrate with the environment and also to protect the environment and life, it doesn't matter how big or small the action what it counts to carry on that action, which it will give not only an example as it also it gives provide an opportunity to life growth and create an important chain that it will prevail in time.

About the Author

Fatima K. Hosein has developed her professional career in the areas of law and education, as well as a special interest in other areas.

www.ingramcontent.com/pod-product-compliance
Lightning Source LLC
LaVergne TN
LVHW022053200926
848481LV00003B/889
* 9 7 9 8 2 3 0 3 6 6 6 6 9 *